Galavanting Goddess:
Alaska to Cuba and Back

Chronicles of a life well-lived

Lisa Ruoff

Printed in the United States of America
First Printing, 2021

ISBN 978-1-7370494-0-1 (paperback)
ISBN 978-1-7370494-1-8 (eBook)

Published by Lisa Ruoff LLC
231 Overlook Dr, Durango CO 81301
www.lisaruoff.com

Cover art by Aria Flis-Chen
Cover design by Zoe Goldberg

Introduction

Having been called many things in my life, neither boring nor conventional ever made it to that list. Swimming for my life from hippos in Lake Malawi. Evading nurse sharks while frolicking under the moon in the coastal waters of Australia. Tying myself to trees to block bulldozers in the forests of Tasmania (okay, so I've made better decisions...). Staring down the barrel of a gun at a border crossing in Zambia. Herding sheep on motorbike in the Outback. Sharing a surprise encounter with a pride of lions in the dark of night while trying to find a place to empty my bladder. Eventually "settling down" to live off the grid in an Alaskan cabin, and then becoming a professional chef/restauranteur in the mountains of Colorado. Definitely not run-of-the-mill stuff for a girl from south Jersey. I'm not sure how I got the travel bug. And I know my family thinks I lost my marbles a long time ago. But there's no denying that somewhere along the way, in my early years, that bug dug in pretty deep!

Travel changes how we view the world. Well, maybe a few years back, I would have said travel and hallucinogens, and although those definitely helped in their own way, I'll stick with just travel for the time being. Being out of your comfort zone. Not knowing the language. Not understanding the currency. Feeling vulnerable. This unease rips apart walls that were constructed in childhood by well-intentioned adults in our lives. Different ways of being and fresh assaults on the senses, to a big part of our population, are considered bad, a threat to our way of life. Our job, as evolving humans, is to deconstruct these walls in order to expand our horizons. To understand other ways of being besides our own. To enjoy new experiences, instead of fearing them. And to understand where that fear may have come from and how to overcome it.

I was traveling around South Africa, just a few years after Nelson Mandela had taken over Presidency. After fifty years of apartheid, there were areas where it was quite volatile and unsafe for whites, and for good reason. After a long day of riding on public transport out of Cape Town, the bus finally stopped at my destination. I was so looking forward to enjoying this local, seaside village. However, a quick assessment of my surroundings clarified I was the only white person, and woman no less, in the visible vicinity. It was not a good situation for me to enter. Energetically, it felt like every cell in my body was screaming, "Do NOT get off this bus right now!" It simply wasn't safe for me. I paid attention to my intuition and stayed put on the bus. Because of that experience, I realized how utterly important it is that every single person on the planet should know the feeling of being a minority. For, in that moment, for maybe the first time in my life, I understood my privilege. And how these people had felt for generations. Generations! In that moment, I understood they had every right to hate me simply for my skin color. If something had happened to me at the hands of that crowd, it would have been the fault of all the white people who had left their imprint before me. It only took a minute... And it changed how I saw the world for the rest of my life. These circumstances, or growth opportunities as I like to call them, rarely happen when confined in the safety of your own comfort zone.

Travel is a rocket boost to embracing different perspectives and other ways of being. It is essential to get out of your comfort zone and overcome your fear of change in order to live life to its fullest. At least, for me it is.

I prefer to travel solo. I've met up with many travelers who started their adventures with friends as companions, only to find that their travel styles didn't quite match. And then the friendship faltered as well as the travel arrangement. Maybe I'm a bit of a loner. Maybe I just couldn't find anyone as crazy as me to join me. For whatever reason, solo traveling has always been my preferred method. I get to call the shots of my experience and hang out with whoever I like. Being a solo female traveler has had its challenges, and I've had to learn over the years to keep my wits about me and entertain a ton of common sense. But being a woman, alone, has given me a personal and singularly female perspective of a dominantly male arena. I wouldn't change it for the world!

I've also found that telling my stories brings a sort of magic along to the listener. Maybe by sharing my personal tales, some young woman may become empowered to live her dream. Or an older, wiser, retiree becomes emboldened to branch out of her comfort zone to engage in an adventure that she wouldn't normally have considered. Maybe not, but if there's any chance that my words may inspire someone to fulfill their soul on a deeper level, I will keep sharing.

The Galavanting Goddess Chronicles are journal entries saved from my worldly adventures, as well as memories never written but held dear in the hippocampus of my brain. The plan is to keep sharing these experiences, through a series of books, as long as they keep happening. Hopefully, they won't stop until my soul moves along to the next realm!

August 13, 2000
Homer, Alaska

The café has been weighing heavy on my mind. It's been over 2 years now since Deb and I had such great sister-time putting the finishing touches on it before the grand opening of The Crescent Moon Café. Those times seem so far away now... Having her take a month out of her life to come up here to Homer, the end of the road as it's known in these parts of Alaska, from Colorado. We had so much fun building out this empty strip-mall space to become a quaint, commercial kitchen and getting our hands dirty and beat up by the tools of the trade. And during what little time we took off to have fun, I got to show her this whimsical little town of Homer that I now call home. Especially during the winter! That was a fantastic month for us sisters. It has been wonderful to get to know the locals through the café - nourishing their bodies with delicious and nutritious food. Then going across the parking lot to the DownEast Saloon for a few beers after closing shop for the day. It even became better when my friend Hank bought the laundromat next door, and we got to spend more time together and share business highs and lows. And I remember how Josh used to come and help me during busy lunch hours, when our relationship was first starting. That doesn't really happen anymore, with all of his time being taken over at the Ranger's station across the bay. Moving his way up the ladder to a full time Ranger and dealing with the State Park doesn't give him much time to be helping me at the café anymore.

Over the past 6 months, I've gotten lonely and bored running this café all by myself. It's all become kind of pointless, and I have little focus anymore. The small space which I thought was so perfect is actually very limiting for growth, and loneliness weighs heavy on me here by myself, day in and day out. Having an employee come in to help for a few days a week is good for a break now and then, but it certainly doesn't lend to camaraderie or bonding in the workplace. Financially, things are going okay with business, but emotionally I'm just not attached anymore.

My relationship has been weighing heavy on my mind, as well. With Josh doing two-week stays at a time across Kachemak Bay at the Ranger's station, and me having to be at the café even when he does finally get some time at home, it really puts a lot of stress on us. Or at least me, anyway. He seems to be fine with being gone all the time. And never really wants to help with my stuff when he is around. It seems so disconnected. I know that this is how things are up here in Alaska for a lot of couples. The women, mostly strong and independent, running businesses in town and the men working up on the oil fields or out on fishing boats. It's hard for me to feel like I'm in an intimate relationship when my partner is never around. I mean, if we're not sharing things, what's the point of being in a relationship? It confuses me, this situation.

I guess my life has been wearing thin on me lately. I'm tired of not being happy. I'm tired of always wanting more. Of feeling like I have to pay my penance before I get to do something that makes my soul sing. And I'm tired of being tired of it all.

Realistically, I know my psyche is panicking about going into the fall season. Winters up here are rough! There is beauty in the moose roaming freely through the snow and the abundance of bald eagles on the Homer spit, and of course, the Northern Lights are always amazing. Those things are my lifelines in the winter. Unfortunately for me, in the winter, the cons outweigh the pros. The dark, damp, cold that seems to descend for months at a time and never go away. The isolation of being in this tiny town at the end of the road, way up North, in the tundra, where the people would rather hide out in their cabins than be social. In the summer, living in a little cabin in the woods with no running water and a wood stove for heat is incredible, and I love it! But in the winter, it's a completely different beast. The dark that starts descending in October descends like an oppressive, damp blanket. Having to rely on an outhouse in the winter can be brutal. Business always slows to a snail's pace, and money gets tight. The locals, those few that I can actually call friends, anyway, seem to disappear into their own little worlds of isolation. It's hard, winter in rural Alaska. It fucks with my head and heart. For these reasons, a lot of the town's population gets out of here for a few months in the winter. Some head for the lower 48. Some head for Hawaii. Others use it as an excuse to go visiting friends or family in warmer, sunnier places. It's completely understandable, given the realities of winter life up here. The beauty and magical crackling of the Northern lights can only take one so far before the dark, cold climate overtakes the soul.

***

Sailing. I've been thinking a lot about sailing. The ocean intimidates me, in an awe-inspiring-fear-based sort of way. And the only way to overcome a fear is to face it. But not here. Not in Alaska. No cold water sailing. Even though there would be ample opportunity for me to get on a local boat down at the harbor and learn the basics. No, I'm envisioning palm trees. Blue-green, sparkling, clear, WARM water. Palm trees along the coast. Suntanned body perched at the bow of a boat. Just the right amount of wind in the sails. Jumping into the crystal clear, WARM sea to frolic at will.

On a more realistic note, the idea of learning to sail a boat is intriguing. I imagine that it's quite a frightening yet empowering undertaking. The one-ness with the ocean must verge on overwhelming.

Then there are my unfounded fears of what lies beneath the surface. Even as a kid, I loved to go to the beach. But I was always moving my feet around, just in case any pinchy, sticky, grotesque creature might find them interesting! If I'm living at sea, I'll have to deal with that. Get over it. Move on. Or how about embrace those pinchy, sticky, grotesque creatures and turn them into allies. Who knows?? I think I may be ready to embark on this new adventure...

August 14

My dreams, now and then, when I can remember them clearly, show me it is possible to live in beauty, love, and light. Sometimes beyond anything I could ever imagine. Like last night, my dreamtime escapades comprised meeting a large, burly, bearded, Viking man. For a brief moment, we were sharing the deliciousness of eating cherry tomatoes on a bench by the harbor. The smell of salt and the sound of seagulls made the vision even more realistic, almost lucid. This Viking was full of vim, vigor, and vitality, and he made everything around him seem somehow lighter, almost sparkly. His smile was contagious, and when he ultimately left me sitting there on the bench, headed for his boat that was tied up to the dock, my heart yearned to have more of his ethereal lightness. I awoke with the vivid memory of his contagious smile, and my entire day was uplifted because of it. There were also some rollerblades in there somewhere, but I wrote those off as a very impertinent bit of information for my brain!

In another dream, I was fortuitous in my meeting of an older woman in a well-cared for veggie garden. She exuded warmth and love, and I was explicably drawn to her. On her head was a floppy hat which kept the harsh sun from her eyes, and a long, flowing skirt swirled softly around her legs. She had a slight essence of a fairy, really, and her very persona was magnetic. My memory of her upon awakening made me yearn to be like her later in my life.

Unfortunately, my experience is that actual life is not like the dreamworld. Not that the actual world is always terrible, or that people are always terrible, but that reality somehow has less magic than dreams. Maybe that's my work. To find the magic in everyday life. To glimpse the smiling, cherubic Viking in the grumpy old man waiting in line at the market, or to see beyond the nastiness of the postal lady to the hidden glimpse of her inner fairy. We all have some sort of spark that has diminished; that life has slowly beaten out of us, unaware of the decline that's even happening. The bitterness that somehow wins out over joyous celebration. To find the magic in everyday life again... That's the whole point, right? Somehow to make magic from gray, foreboding clouds.

August 16
Homer, AK

I pray to the Universe for me to have patience not only with those in my life, and those unknown to me, but most of all with myself. Somehow, I have created a very isolated existence that I don't always wish to be a part of. I don't wish to be alone or lonely, but somehow, I always seem to find that solitary place. I know that there is a reason for this, but time and time again, I am placed here, or I create this place in front of me. I know there must be something here I can and must gain from. I only wish to understand and grasp whatever that thing is and move on. Hopefully move forward into a place filled with loving and caring people who wish to be there with me. I ask for assistance from all the beings and energies to please help me break out of this solitary path.

August 22, 2000

Last night I took Boomer out for a walk. It was a dreary, wet night, and I really didn't want to go out in the rain, but he kept giving me those pathetic, puppy dog eyes, and I couldn't help but to cave to his wishes. About five minutes into the walk, I took my hat and coat off and let the rain soak me. Alaska weather rarely allows the luxury of enjoying warm rain. The rain here is usually a bone chilling 40 degrees. But this temperate rain felt fabulous, soaking me through to my skin and making my hair drip into my eyes. I couldn't help but think about how long it's been since I've described something as feeling wonderful. My relationship hasn't. My café hasn't. I haven't.

***

It's been over two years now since I met Josh on that rainy day in the woods. A torrential downpour had been overtaking my little campsite for a few hours by that point, and my tent was becoming an island amongst the forming streams in my beautiful, unfrequented spot in the wilds of Kachemak Bay State Park. The barking of my trusty watchdog, Boomer, alerted me to fellow humans nearby. Peeking out of my drenched island oasis, I spotted two rain-gear-clad forest dwellers headed my way. Josh and his trail crew companion saw my tent and checked in to make sure its inhabitant was doing okay in the soaking conditions. And that is how I met him, my current "partner." Over 2 years ago... It seems like decades.

After a few weeks of heated discussions about him taking a job on Kodiak Island for a month or more, despite my dislike of this "opportunity," as he called it, he has left. This was definitely not a joint decision. I was not invited in any way and this was solely his choice against my wishes. Once again, this is not my idea of an ideal relationship: being with someone who is never around. I'm not really sure when or if he's coming back. And I'm not entirely sure that I care. I'm beginning to think that I'm going to spend the rest of my life very lonely. Maybe not alone, but lonely. I set my standards way too high.

But then again, are they? Is it me? Or haven't I found the right one yet? Being a female Scorpio has its challenges, and relating to others is one of them. We Scorpios are always looking for ways to go deeper in our connections with others. I want to share my SOUL with my partner, not only my time. Most men don't understand what that even means, and Josh is no exception. If it were up to him, we would have gotten married already. But it's not. And we aren't. So, it IS me. I know my needs aren't simple. But it seems that I simply can't get my needs met. I want to get lost when I look into someone's eyes. At least once in a while, lightning bolts are a necessity to stir things up. I don't think I can live without some level of passion. I don't have that now.

What I have is a very good man who is not my soul mate. And it leaves me confused and unfulfilled.

August 25, 2000

Working on some possibilities today. After giving this sailing idea some more thought, I scrutinized it a bit closer and put some feelers out there. After speaking with some people who have ties to the sailing world, I am finding that there are many aspects of this world that are completely new to me. I'm wanting to get involved with the sailors who are live-aboards, also known as cruisers. These are the people who have left their land dwelling lives, their spacious houses with sprawling lawns and gardens, to live on a boat. A tiny space that is constantly in motion. Usually a sailboat. Sailing becomes their life. The idea is very intriguing.

I found a sailing magazine based out of San Francisco called Latitude 38 that focuses on the cruising lifestyle and put a classified ad in it for "crew available." Seems plausible to get on a cruiser sailboat and trade my time and efforts for the opportunity to learn how to sail. It might be a long shot, but I gotta start flowing the energy in some sort of direction!

September 3

After many highly emotional pleas for attention and many heartfelt conversations about the state of our relationship, Josh and I have finally shifted it to solely friendship. His choice to take this remote job, with no consideration of my wants or needs, made it very clear to me we don't share the same idea of an ideal relationship. The Josh saga seemed to work itself into the space it needs to be right now. No bitter or harsh feelings. A bit of heartache and pain mixed up in there. But I feel it is the right decision. We just weren't making each other happy. More to the point, we weren't even there for each other. He's busy with his end of the summer stuff at the Ranger's station, and I'm busy trying to figure out my next step. Then he leaves for Kodiak Island for a month or more, and that leaves me to make my own decisions about my future. Neither of us has the time or energy to give to the other right now. And that's not fair to either of us. So, friends it is... Time to pick up the pieces of my heart and create a new existence. Now to decide what to do about the café...

September 7

I feel like a new person! It's like once I went with the flow instead of against it; it's all exciting and energizing! Four days left and the café will be closed. I needed the clarity of where I stand in relation to Josh. And I feel GREAT. The difference is that I'm not seeing any of it as an ending, but as another opportunity for a new beginning. I was driving down the road yesterday, and I felt like crying. Not from sadness or grief, but more for appreciation to myself and the Universe for giving me so much.

There are many people in my life that care for me, love me, and help me. I'm surrounded by so much love. It's really a matter of me noticing it and appreciating it instead of taking it for granted. I guess I've been wanting it so badly in my relationship with Josh that when I stopped focusing on what he wasn't giving me, I noticed everyone else waiting to help me and appreciate me. I really DO have all that I need, plus some to spare.

This change in perception has opened up my capacity for some long-lost friends as well. I am so fortunate to have made strong bonds with people from all over the world because of having the experiences I've had. One of those friends, Sooz, called from Australia yesterday and really gave me a boost. I haven't spoken with her in a long time. It was actually her and her ex that gave me the base to move to Alaska from Colorado. Spending time with them in Anchorage when I first drove up here was a fantastic few weeks and opened my eyes to the beauty of Alaska. They let me and my trusty four-legged beast live there until I got my bearings and moved to Homer. While Boomer and I were living in a tent for the summer, we would make trips up to the big city to visit Sooz and

Marcel (her ex) regularly. Unfortunately, Marcel had an affair with someone else and they broke off their 2-year relationship. I guess it was about 6 months ago or so that she moved back to her parents' house in Australia. Anyway... she gave me a contact number for a conservation society in Panama that accepts volunteers to help with their work for sea turtles. And today I found a website for a place in Cameroon accepting volunteers to help on a chimpanzee sanctuary. I mean, holy shit! How cool would that be? I called the number on their website, and they told me to fax my resume to them ASAP. That's top priority for tomorrow...

Here's to new beginnings!

September 8, 20000

I've been enjoying my time with lots of friends, which I never even noticed that I had, along with all the people associated to the café. Even went on a freebie bear viewing flight with my friends/business connections, Chris and Ken, for a day across Cook Inlet. Throughout the summer, they would call me up at the café to deliver charter lunches to their customers to take on their bear viewing excursions. Through our business connection, a sort of friendship developed. This is the second time they have called me at the last minute to fill an empty seat in one of their tours across the inlet. Super cool! And so grateful to them for offering me such a sublime experience.

They're a great couple, those two... Him being all big and burly, and her being a slight little thing. Both of them always seem so jovial. Yes, jovial—that's the word for them! They are the quintessential story of the couple that moved to Alaska in their youth and found their hearts in the mountains and oceans of this wild place. They've been here for over 20 years now and make their living taking tourists into the Alaskan wilderness to view brown bears (popularly known as grizzlies) in their natural habitat.

There were five other people on the tour with us, and when Ken landed the float plane on the lake across the inlet, everyone was riveted to what Chris had to tell us before heading off into the tundra in search of 1000-plus-pound brown bears (in AK, we call them brown bears, not grizzlies). This little blonde woman, possibly all 5 feet of her, standing in the front of the ten-seat pontoon plane in the middle of a remote lake, with a rifle slung across her shoulder almost the same size as her tiny frame, certainly demanded all of our attention and respect! She leads the hikes, and Ken takes up the rear, making sure that no one lags behind and that the group stays together. After being told the rules of the turf (how to not get eaten by a grizzly), we were off. All in one obedient brief line behind our brave, tiny, rifle-slinging guide! It's an utterly awe-inspiring feeling to know that you're out there, in the middle of the wilderness—no roads, no houses, no other humans—sharing this beautiful space with a bunch of enormous carnivores who really couldn't care less about your presence. During salmon season, these beautiful and possibly deadly giants engorge themselves on the swimming delicacies in the stream. Although there was one point during the day that had my heart racing. For some reason, Chris had taken a step back from the lead, which left me as the frontrunner. We were all trudging through the shallows of the alpine stream, and there were salmon everywhere underfoot, when I looked up and saw a brown bear, about six or seven hundred pounds, running straight at me. I froze in my tracks. Instantly, I believe my heart stopped dead. I saw my life flash before my eyes. The bear came to an abrupt stop about 50 yards in front of me, busy with its catch of a salmon snack. HOLY MOTHER OF GOD!!! When my heart started beating again, it just about jumped out of my chest. I wasn't sure if I wanted to laugh hysterically or throw up, or both.

There's a well-told joke in Alaska –
"When a bear is charging you, just throw shit in its face."
"But, where do you get the shit, you ask?"
"If a brown bear is charging you, I guarantee there will be a pile of shit at your feet!"
True dat!!! Holy shit!

September 10

Only a few more days of delivering charter lunches to the Spit, and that'll be the end of the café. Funny, when I conjured up the charter lunch aspect of the café business, it somehow didn't quite register precisely how early a 5:30 am delivery is. Since the lunches are made the night before, it's not an all-night ordeal in the kitchen. Which is better than nothing, I guess. After a few summers, I have found that once I'm up and going, it's actually quite beautiful and peaceful getting to the docks before anyone else is around. Enjoying the sunrise over Kachemak Bay before it becomes busy with boats and activity. Considering that sunrises in the summer here are pretty freaking early, that's saying a lot!

The naptime between my deliveries and the opening of the café was always a welcome time of day. Handing off the packed lunches to all the tourists headed out on their fishing charters for the day has pretty much kept the café coffers filled throughout the summer.

After my second wake-up, seeing as how I didn't have to go back to open for the day, I laid in the sun in my undies until I got a chill. Ha! I guess I can consider myself a true Alaskan now. 48 degrees and I'm so excited about the "nice weather" that I'm outside basically naked! Now I have come a bit more to my senses and am on the back deck in a few more layers. A much more prudent fashion statement for 48 degrees...

***

I feel good, besides the leftover alcohol in my system from last night. I mean, my soul and spirit feel good. It's been a few weeks now that I've been basking in this lightness of being. Socially, it's like a door opened and I am now flooded with abundance. Physically, I feel healthy and fit and think I look good too. Financially, the café ended up with more money in the account than I was expecting, with only a few more days of charter lunch deliveries until the ultimate end. Emotionally, it's had lots of ups and downs, but more ups.

Admittedly, it has been a point of contention between Earl, the landlord, and I over the closing of the café. As the first renter in the space, I built it out to be a legally licensed kitchen from a concrete slab without even walls. There was a lot of time and money put into the infrastructure that came directly from my pocket. He wants me to tear it all apart to take the kitchen out and make it back into the original retail space I rented it as. My point is, that it would be much more appealing to rent as a commercial kitchen. He could even charge more for it, if he wanted to. But he seems to disagree and wants me to rip it all apart. So that's going to be a bit of a job. Who knows? It could be extremely validating to take a sledgehammer to things right now. Maybe good for my head space. I have to see it as a positive thing and not let it get to me too much.

Selling all the café stuff has gone over very well so far, and it seems like I may put away more money than I expected towards whatever the next adventure may be.

Not sure that Cameroon is a viable option, really, but I still sent them my resume. And I'm looking into some more volunteer opportunities in Central America, as well. I'm really focusing on this sailing idea. It's sounding more and more appealing to me. There really are so many options and opportunities. But one step at a time. Gotta tie up all these loose ends around my Alaskan life first.

Early October is a trip to New Orleans with the family women. I think there will be about 6 of us for a long weekend. And sometime before then, I would like to go across the bay and help Josh for a while, winterizing the Ranger's station over there. Possibly camping for a few nights before it gets too arctic. It's a good time of year to be over there. No tourists and an entire state park to ourselves. Even though we moved our relationship away from the intimate partnership that it was, I still have faith that we can actually move into the friend-zone with some sort of grace and ease.

God, it all feels so GOOD! Life can really be amazing if you choose to make it that way. I'm so thankful that I never sold out for a "normal" reality!

Sept 25

Well, it's really over. The café is closed. I have ripped out all the walls, and the plumbing has been torn apart and taken out. I have finished the irrevocable steps. And my first reaction was to cry, cry, cry. I lost it! I cried and cried, then went out to lunch with my friends Steve and Noelle, and cried some more. After that, I got drunk with Hank. Noelle has been a good friend for a few years and understands that I can be pretty emotional over bigger life situations such as this. Steve, however, is a newly gained friendship, and he was a bit more at a loss for how to be a support for me. His career as a social worker makes him a very empathetic and attentive listener, though. And, of course, good old Hank is always there for me to lean on whenever I need him! Since our connecting as mutual entrepreneurs when he took over the laundromat next door to the café, we have been the closest of friends. He being a very conservative, older redneck, and I being the young, tree-hugging, hippie chick is quite the mismatched friendship, but it works for us.

I was a mess, all crying and snotty and emotional. But it was nice to have a few shoulders to lean on.

And now I'm trying to figure out where, what, and when? Once again, the same situation thrown in my face. Once again, it's my own doing. Today, I felt like a failure. Just a few years ago, I remember feeling so energized about the new business. Having Deb here for a few weeks to help build out the space and put the finishing touches on it was so connected, refreshing, and inspiring. Smoking dope and painting to the smooth and soulful tunes of Van Morrison and Frank Sinatra. Cooking a huge Xmas dinner as a dry run for the menu. And binge cooking for 24 hours in order to have everything ready for opening on New Year's Day. It was all so new, so exciting, so joyful. And then I had to rip it all apart again. Like an autopsy after a surprise and curious death. But what was I searching for, ripping down that drywall and tearing out that plumbing? The only reason I can find for the death of that café is me. They say that every failure is actually a success in disguise, but it certainly doesn't feel that way right now. It's painful and demoralizing. My heart aches, my dreams destroyed. And my eyes are going to be puffy for days. Goodbye, Crescent Moon Café. Thank you for all the good times and memories. New beginnings, old endings, different phases, more possibilities, all over again. Different timing, back to the old me... It's time to put on my big girl panties and get on with the show.

October 9, 2000

Returned from a long weekend last night after a fast and furious time in New Orleans with the family women last night. What a laugh! Even though we all have our differences, and I exited the family fold years ago, I feel a new acceptance of us all as individuals in a family. Fewer judgements, and a lot more acceptance. It's a very welcome change, and I appreciate it.

Deb and I met up the night before everyone else arrived and had a wander in the French Quarter. Drank a few Hurricanes and saw some live music. Plenty of drugs to be had if we wanted them! Every 20 feet, it seemed, we were being propositioned by yet another passerby on the street. No partaking for us, though. No thanks. It's been a while since I indulged in any of that stuff, and I'm certainly not going to start up again by buying god-only knows-what from some dealer off the street in the French Quarter!

At one point we stopped at a grimy, but somehow welcoming, doorway to check out a happy, funky, upbeat band. And they were phenomenal! There was a guy playing the washboard - the quintessential scene - sexy, very fit, tall, young, black man with the most amazing blue eyes. Even at 40 feet away, we could clearly appreciate his eyes. They were the color of the ocean off the coast of some deserted island in the South Pacific. Magically mesmerizing... The washboard hung over his neck and covered his entire chest as he strummed away at it with a spoon. Holy shit, he was smokin'! And he knew it too. Ah, New Orleans, how you easily carve a bit of yourself into my heart.

The next day the rest of the fam arrived, and we all had a blast together. My mother being the matriarch of the bunch, five sisters, and two very close family friends made for scenes full of obscenely loud laughter and lots of intoxication. A family of varied middle age women set loose on the unsuspecting city of New Orleans—great fun! Obviously, a good dose of alcohol certainly helps with greasing the wheels of the family machinery.

And now, back to my previously scheduled life antics.

10/14/00

My friend, Colleen, and I were talking the other day and got the proverbial ball rolling. Colleen and I got to know each other through Josh and the State Park. I remember the early days of our friendship, when Josh and I had just started dating, while he was both working and living in the same building—the Ranger's Station. Colleen worked in the upstairs office of the station, and she and I would waste time chatting while I was waiting for Josh to get his miscellaneous paperwork done between work stays at the

Ranger's stations in Homer and his work stints across the bay in Halibut Cove.

On our recurring date for Mexican food last week, I was telling her about all my possibilities, the most appealing one being sailing. Of course, as it so happens, her recent ex, Jim, has a sailboat in dry dock down in Mexico. He's currently planning on heading down there to fix it up and get it in the water. Like, as in, within the next week. She introduced us, and low and behold, both of our plans, or at least my willingness for pretty much anything right now, fit together perfectly. The timing is good. Our personalities seem to work together well. Our mutual admiration of tequila (just kidding, sort of!) helps. Jim bought a travel trailer that goes on the back of his pickup truck, so we can camp out along the way. So it is.

We leave within the next few days. Acquiring provisions, outfitting the camper, gathering music for the road, and other such travel preparations have encompassed my past few days. It's been glorious! A road trip from Homer AK to the Baja in Mexico with the focus of getting Jim's 38-foot Hans Christian sailboat into the water and sailing.

The only part that is questionable, of course, is the aspect of mutual attraction. We have not confronted it, this somewhat uncomfortable pink elephant, but I believe that both Jim and I are curiously dancing around the issue to see how it will play out. Just go with it, or not... Yet another great opportunity for me to simply TRUST. Trust in the process. Trust that the Universe will guide me (us) in the right direction. And have fun in the meantime. My friendship with Colleen has no bearing on this possible romantic infliction, since she left Jim for another guy who is much more into her than Jim ever seemed to be. Or so I'm told...

As if I needed more synchronicity to this whole situation, Colleen is currently looking for a place to rent, because of her moving out of Jim's cabin, so she is going to take over the remaining time on the lease of my rental cabin and take care of my furry buddy, Boomer, while I'm away on the adventure. I know she loves animals and will be a fantastic surrogate mom to my fur baby. So. Freaking. Perfect.

Once again, in great gratitude to the Universe...

October 20/00 (or so)
Roslyn, WA

Ohhhhhh.... It's a rough one this morning... We stopped in a little town in northern Washington state last night called Roslyn. This is where the filming of the show Northern Exposure took place. So, we wanted to indulge ourselves and check it out. The downtown bar was great. Good drinks and food, some live music, and a lot of fun. Obviously, a bit too much fun. Waking up in the camper this morning is slow going. My head is throbbing, and I think I might puke. Trying really hard NOT to puke, actually! Jim is finding this all very amusing, much to my chagrin. But the rig must keep rolling, so I will stick my head out the window for most of this morning's driving adventures, I'm sure. Ugh....

Later

Okay, I made it. I didn't puke and now am getting somewhat back to a normal state of mind and body. The start of the trip was fast and furious. Once Jim and I decided it was a go, it WENT! Getting the cabin space ready for Colleen, setting up the camper for the trip, and basically situating ourselves to leave our lives for a few months. It's been really fun to share the excitement of an adventure with someone who is just as excited. Josh and I were good together, but we never really shared the excitement of traveling adventures. Actually, now that I think of it, I don't think I've ever shared the excitement of travel adventures with a man. Wow, that says a lot. I guess that's not so true, though. Josh and I shared a bunch of road trips together. But it never felt like excitement with him. It was always very practical. Simply a well-planned trip we had to make by car. Weird. Well, I'm changing that story!

***

The AlCan, as it's called (the Alaska-Canada highway), runs through one of the most remote and untouched areas of the northern hemisphere. Not sure of the exact starting and ending points of the route, but I know it's over 1500 miles long. Although most people would call the area desolate, I think it's the epicenter of where all things begin. The "middle of nowhere" to me is really the center of everywhere! Nothing, and I mean no trace of human interaction with nature (besides the highway, of course) can be witnessed. Just nature in all of her untouched glory. It's hard to imagine if you've seen nothing like it. The gas stations are so far apart that every vehicle on that stretch of road has extra gas cans. It's not a place you want to break down! But the views, the wildlife, the serenity... It's as close to God as I could ever imagine being - and I don't use the term God often! If she does exist, I'm certain she can be found out there in the wilderness somewhere.

We made a brief stop at some hot springs we stumbled upon in the Yukon. It was a surreal and majestic setting. The air temp was cold enough that the condensation had formed crystals that covered the area around the warm pools. And, of course, there wasn't another person anywhere in sight. After our private hot springs session, I decided to take advantage of nature's bounty of warm water and wash my hair. Actually, Jim offered, and I accepted. I laid down, face up, on a nearby picnic table while Jim carefully rinsed and washed my hair with buckets of hot water from the springs. It was a kind and intimate act that only lasted a few minutes but would stay with me for years. If you're ever looking to make a great first impression, I highly recommend washing someone's hair with natural hot springs water from a Yukon spring while laying on a picnic table! Good move, Jim.

The status of our relationship was a bit of an uncertainty for a moment. Honestly, I wasn't even really sure I wanted it to be anything more than friendship. But that has sorted itself out, as it usually does! How could I possibly turn down a romantic tryst whilst traipsing from state to state via camper on our way to a sailing excursion in Mexico?? I couldn't. I'm not. The game is very much on!

October 22, 2000
Oregon Coast

Heavenly sand in our toes and ocean breezes through our hair makes for two very grateful traveling souls. We got here last night, to this Northern California beach, just in time to see a beautiful sunset, all bright pinks and light purples. Took a walk on the beach which is bordered by a large stretch of rolling sand dunes with white, soft sand. I couldn't help but to sleep out under the stars. It couldn't have been more perfect—a bottle of wine, warm sleeping bag, both of us nestled together in the sand dunes, the sound of the waves crashing nearby, stars twinkling above (we counted ten shooting stars!), and good conversation. Considering the brisk temps last night, there was no partaking of carnal pleasures, which we both willingly made up for this morning. After rousing from the sleeping bags, it was time for us to enjoy coffee and chai tea on the beach, watching the seabirds and letting the soul-nourishing sounds of the gently breaking waves wash over us both. I partook of some yoga on the beach with an inquisitive seal peering from the waves while Jim took the liberties of making the most of our isolated haven by jogging down the beach in nothing but his birthday suit. Life does not suck right now...

A few days ago, on our way through Oregon, we took a day and did some wine tasting. I learned that wines grown in cooler, more humid climates certainly have a different palate than what most people are used to. I mean, it was wine, so I liked it—ha! But it wasn't my favorite. I guess my palate is a bit more used to the taste of a struggling, dry/hot climate grape. Wow, listen to me turning into a wine snob after a day of wine tasting in back country Oregon vineyards.

Today is our day off from driving, and so far, I'm hot and wearing a sarong in the warm sunshine. Sand in my toes, sun on my face, sea salt on my body–we're not in Alaska anymore, boys and girls! It's astonishing to me how utterly different my energy has changed since a few short weeks ago. The memory of my recent breakdown and the feeling of complete and utter failure because of the deconstruction of the café has completely shifted into total freedom, abundance, and gratitude in my current reality. I'm not sure what kind of longevity this connection with Jim will offer, but for now, I am letting it all soak in and fill me up! Tomorrow, it's back on the road.

10/28/00
35,000 feet in the Air

Holy Shit! So much energy flowing in all directions... Tomorrow is the celebration of the ending of my 29th year here on this planet. A year from the big 3-0. I guess I should feel older, possibly wiser. But I'm up to my same old antics. Currently, I am somewhere between Chicago and Florida in the air on my way to Ft. Lauderdale. The road trip from Alaska to Mexico got sidetracked somewhere in California. Go figure! In Oregon, Jim got a call to go back to work for about a five-week stretch. I think it was somewhere in central America that needed his tugboat captain skills this time around. So, after a few wonderful days spent deliciously wasting time on white, sandy beaches, we made it down to Phoenix in a lot less time than we planned. He flew out from there, and I visited with an old roommate of mine from the Colorado days, Jen and her husband Mike, for a few days. Fortunately for me, my friends are outstanding and they let me keep my snowboarding and biking stuff that I had been carting around in the camper in their garage. Which freed me up to go explore other adventures unhindered. Just me and my backpack like the good old days!

***

There were actually a few legit responses from the ad I put out in that sailing magazine for "crew available." I was unaware of all the single men out there looking for a young, cute, available "crew" member to help them sail off into the sunset. It's curious how important a crew member's measurements seem to be. Hmmm...!

Anyway, I got in touch with one responder–who didn't ask me my dimensions. He says he has a chef job on a boat out of Ft. Lauderdale. The plan is that this guy, Gary, will pick me up at the airport in Ft. Lauderdale when I land, and I can stay in the extra room at his place while we get things situated.

So there ya go! Another side trip on the travel schedule. Energy goes where attention flows. A little shift in perception, and here I am, following the latest stream to yet another watershed!!

Now I'm sitting here, on the plane, trying to create the rest of that reality. I would love to get on a boat doing whale or dolphin conservation down in the Caribbean or somewhere similar, but I can't really conjure up any images specifically. I guess I'll have to stay open to all possibilities and see where the flow takes me. That really hasn't been a problem lately.

Still no word from Josh. I hoped we could remain close after the breakup, but I'm leaving that ball in his court. I miss sharing with him. But I have to give him space. After speaking with some mutual friends, I know that he's up in Girdwood, AK and has gotten a cell phone now. My heart knows that he is living his best life, spending his winter time off from the State Park to be a ski instructor at Alyeska Resort. At least his new single status releases him of those necessary family visits that he dealt with so agreeably last winter. Now he gets to be selfish and do what he loves to do, which is play in the snow. We all deserve to do what we love. Happiness, joy, and wellness are what I wish for him.

11/2/00
Ft. Lauderdale, FL

This moment finds me laying on the beach in Ft. Lauderdale. The last few days have been odd, at best. Gary was waiting for me at the baggage claim when I landed. The sun had already set by the time we got into his car, which I found out later was really his parents' car, and headed for his apartment, also not his but his parents. He seemed like a nice enough guy. Maybe over-exuberant, but harmless. Although, as we were driving down the highway, the thought crossed my mind that I'm a complete idiot. Here I am, with some guy I don't know, in a place I'm not familiar with, driving to stay at some apartment I've never been to. Oh, fucking BRILLIANT, Lis...! Splendid position to put yourself in. At that moment, my options were to trust the process or jump out of a moving car on a highway at night in a place I don't know. So, keep on going...

Turns out, Gary wasn't the most upfront guy on the planet, which really shouldn't have been a shocker considering we met from a classified ad in a magazine. Duh... He didn't actually have a job for me. Or us, I should say. He needed me to get us a gig. See, the way it works down here is that these mega-super-rich boat owners have boat shows. And that's where us mere peons show up looking for scraps—aka, work. This wasn't really what I had in mind. Being promenaded around for 2 days, kissing ass to the ultra-rich for the hopes of finding employment, has not been what I would call enjoyable. It's like Aspen, but boat style. Owners of eight-million-dollar yachts looking for servants to work for them. Within 20 hours of picking me up from the airport, Gary had me in white boat shoes, tube socks (to hide my tattoo, god forbid...), khaki shorts with a sailor's belt, and a white polo shirt. He even made me take off all my beaded jewelry and had me address these pompous elitists as "captain" or "Mr. and Mrs." Absolutely no first names allowed out of us peons. To say that I was a bit out of my element was a complete understatement! Anyway, we went for an interview the other day for a captain and chef position on a 100-ft Broward yacht. Actually, it's a 90-foot yacht at the moment, in dry dock getting a ten-foot extension put onto it. The retrofit should be done in a month or less. Seriously?!

Meeting the owners at the interview was like glimpsing behind the curtain into a world I never knew existed, nor did I really want to. He is your basic older white male. Overweight in the belly area and a more than slightly receded hairline. She was an older white woman. Lots of makeup. From the looks of it, lots of money spent on plastic surgeons. And a rock the size of a freakin' softball on her left finger. How the hell she holds her hand up under the weight of that thing, who could tell? But they seemed quite nice. Downright likeable, actually. Surprising. Much more likeable than the guy I'm supposed to be living on a boat with for months. During the interview, the "Mr." of the yacht moved to stand up and get coffee. To which Gary quickly told him I would be more than happy to make a fresh pot and fill his cup for him, not to worry and have a seat. At which time, all eyes turned on me expectantly. My insides flopped, and I was instantly seething. How dare he! Fucking male chauvinist asshole! But instead of making a scene, I swallowed my independent warrior woman's pride and rose to the demeaning task at hand. Inwardly cursing Gary the entire time and harboring animosity towards both the Mr. and Mrs. for continuing on with the interview while I was playing servant. It was only by the grace of god that I made it through that interview without exploding. But I did. And we somehow came across as a wonderfully professional sailing/chefing team.

The current scenario is that we're waiting to find out if we get the gig. If so, it entails living on the boat and taking care of it while they are not there. Bringing it to wherever they want it to be when they want to be on it. And taking care of them and their rich friends while on board. Basically, we would get to live on a 100-ft yacht on our own for about half the year while kissing their asses for the other half. The price is right, so I agreed that if we got an offer, I would take it with him. I'm hoping that I made it abundantly clear that this was a business deal. I'm NOT sharing his berth, and we are NOT a couple. If we don't get an offer, I'm outta here!

I kind of hope we don't get an offer because this isn't exactly what I was looking for. I was kinda clueless that this world even existed, really. I wanted to learn how to sail, and this isn't a sailboat. And spending a year in close quarters with someone I have no urge to be intimate with is questionable. But I'm here now, and this is the situation, and the money is pretty spectacular given the circumstances. I mean, where else could I possibly earn a yearly salary while getting to live on a yacht? If I could suck it up for a year, it would be a tremendous help financially. The other side of the coin is six months of living on someone else's yacht, while getting paid, without them there. Spoken in those terms, it doesn't sound so bad...

If we don't get it, I'm planning on heading back to Jen and Mike's place in Phoenix. I can get my stuff and head down to the boatyard in Mexico to pick up with the original plan to help Jim get his sailboat out of dry dock and into the Sea of Cortez. I'm almost certain Mom and Sue are down in the Keys right now. So, I could rent a car and hop out to spend some family time with them. These things all cost money, though. Not including what I recently spent to get here. I mean, I should have a sufficient amount to get me through a few months of adventure, but it's not like I won the lottery!

It's pretty obvious, my current state of confusion. At first, it felt so right to come here. Like it was divine flow. But now I can't figure out what I'm doing here. This millionaire yacht stuff isn't quite what I thought I was manifesting. And I'd much rather be living out the original plan of heading to Mexico with Jim. Ahhhh.... I'm going swimming now and hopefully drown away my confusion.

11/6/00
Sanibel Island, FL

Sitting under a palm tree on a beach on Sanibel island, crying. That's the current update. I keep creating all these things, sometimes to the point of utter chaos. I can't decide on any direction. Gary and I got offered the job on the yacht. And he's completely understanding of my need to keep our relationship business-like and platonic, at least, so he says. The money is significant, and the work seems minimal, at least compared to owning a freaking café! But I don't think I can do it. It's not sitting well with me. What's wrong with me? I create these pretty amazing situations, and then I don't want them. What the fuck???

I'm staying with Sue and Mom for a few days at Sue's rental condo in Sanibel. It's perfect timing that they are here right now. They gave me a great excuse to get the hell out of that situational energy for a day or two. To get my head right again. As usual, my family understands nothing in my world. I can't even really tell them too many details because they already think I'm certifiably nuts. But it is a pleasant reprieve and a good chance to refocus.

I don't think I can do it. I can't bear to think of myself in docksiders and polishing railings for rich people. Especially after how he treated me like such a servant at the interview. There to do his bidding. It's all too much for me to grasp. I'll have to let Gary know he has to find another chef to take my place.

11/10/00

Picked up a book today and read an excerpt that really hit home...

The Wild Woman

"A wild woman is extraordinarily herself. She does what is natural to her without inhibitions, which means she can do and be anything. A wild woman is spontaneous, bold, sexually alive, and takes risks and leaps before she thinks and is willing to express all of herself. She is untamed by herself or others. She says and does what she feels. She can be quiet and thoughtful, fierce and angry. She's joyful, laughs loudly, plays hard, screams and mourns her losses. A wild woman will at times be unsettling to herself and others. She can even be (oh, no!) offensive. She is loved by many, but can be threatening to others. She has discovered her wild nature and is willing to express it. She allows herself to wonder where her wild, fun side has gone – and then allows herself to find out. Wildness is natural."

From "A Whistling Woman Is Up to No Good," by Laurel King

11/13/00
Jacksonville, FL

Monday, November 13–one of my best friends on the planet, Alison's birthday, and I forgot to call her. There are certain constants in life. And talking to Alison on her birthday is one of them. Every year since high school. And I fucked it up. But I sent a card. I hope that makes up for it! Thank God for my friends and their acceptance of me and my idiosyncrasies.

***

It's presently 12:30am, and I am sitting in a Greyhound bus station in Jacksonville, FL. Waiting for the 3 am bus to Wilmington, NC. Jesus Christ, North Carolina?? You never know...

On my way to meet Matt. He's 31 and has his own 39' sailboat and wants some company sailing down the East coast, and then on to the Caribbean islands. It doesn't sound like he has a ton of experience. But he has been building boats for six years, and he just took a three-and-a-half-month single handed sail up to New England and back again. Given that information, I'm assuming he has to know a bit of something! We've been talking and emailing all week, and the vibes are good, much better than with Gary. But just in case, we're going to take it slow along the coast. If it doesn't work out between us, I'll simply jump ship in FL. We'll see... What a crazy adventure this last month has been! Leaving Alaska in search of a sailing experience in Mexican waters–then leaving Phoenix before even reaching Mexico in search of some sailing experience in Ft. Lauderdale–then leaving FL to get away from a guy who was using me to get a job to visit the family in Sanibel Island – then leaving Sanibel to West Palm Beach to visit other friends. And now, en route to North Carolina to venture off on yet another sailing excursion with another unknown male waiting to pick me up. I guess the third time's a charm. First, it was Jim to Mexico. Then Gary in FL. Now Matt in NC. All souls I never would have run into if I hadn't believed in creating my own reality. And all who have touched my soul in their own way, whether it be positive or negative. It's all part of the process. And the story continues...

11/15/2000
North Carolina Coast

Well, I have been trying to create this reality of being on a sailboat for over a month now. And so it is! At this very moment, I'm basking in the sun, contemplating jumping into some cold water, aboard a nicely accommodating 38' Valiant sailboat. Matt, the owner and captain, seems like a nice enough guy. No major bond or lightning, but I think our sailing partnership could work out fine. No romantic interest here, which is sort of refreshing and welcomed right now. Some decent company, and some new sailing skills for me. He's about to take the dinghy and do laundry. So, looks like I'll be alone for a while to deal with my own thoughts.

This morning, we went shopping for provisions and are loaded with goods now. Only bought one bottle of wine, so it looks like I'll be cutting down on the drinking, which is probably a good thing after the major amounts I drank last week while visiting with friends down in Florida! And there's the 10 pounds I've added to my body since leaving Alaska that I wouldn't be sad to see go. Ugh... Anyway, I digress... The boat... Almost sunset and listening to BB King. We're taking off tomorrow to cruise the ICW (InterCoastal Waterway) until Georgetown, SC and then see how the weather is. For now, it looks like a few days of motoring, but then the sails should go up, and that's when I learn to become a sailor! Yippee! That's actually good, because just getting used to everything on the boat is going to be an extensive learning process. Gotta start somewhere. And motoring gives me time to focus on the stuff I'll need to know once the sails actually go up. The ICW, or the ditch, as it's sometimes referred to, is a long, almost canal-like waterway that runs from southern Virginia through Florida. It is a shallow, protected waterway that can be very remote but also intersects with ocean and river passes in very busy areas at points. It's a great way to get some protection from ocean storms. Or in our case, to simply take our time getting to know the ways of the boat and the water before hitting the open ocean.

***

I tried to call both Mom and Deb yesterday, but neither were home and neither has called back yet. Wassup with that?? How rude! Where are they? Aren't they just waiting around, anticipating a much-awaited call from the all-important ME?? Oh well. I'll get over it. There's a bit of satisfaction in knowing that there is not a soul on the planet who knows where I am right now, current company excluded. That makes me smile.

11/18/2000
North Carolina Coast

Peanut butter and crackers... 12:30 pm... just eating... no exercise... sitting on this thing floating in the water... my body getting bigger... clothes getting tighter... Ugh... Gotta stabilize the exercise/food consumption ratio.

This morning was eventful. I almost sank the boat. Oh joy. It was only by some grace of the heavens that water didn't start pouring in through the hull. It all happened within a 30-second period. I am at the helm. Matt's down below having some pancakes or something. We're motoring out in the middle of the river. Nice and wide, about 5 ½ knots on a beautiful but cold day. And suddenly the depth finder drops from 25 to 7 in about five seconds. The alarm beeps its annoying beep, and I slam the throttle down by half instantly. Then—BAM!!!!!!! - the whole boat lurches forward. The bow of the boat almost disappears underwater for a split instant. Things are flying everywhere. I'm standing at the helm, frozen in horror, expecting water to be coming at me from all directions. Then both Matt and I are flying around like headless chickens (I never really saw a headless chicken, but from what I've heard...). We're both just waiting to sink and not knowing what to do about it. By some freak of nature, though, we seem to be unharmed. There was no water rushing in through a gaping hole in the hull. Nothing. Holy SHIT?!!? How did we get so fortunate???

Matt thinks we hit a tree or some sort of log that was unseen, barely under the surface. God, I felt horrible! My first time alone at the helm, and I slam the boat into something unseen! I'm not so sure Matt has much confidence in me right now, and I can't really blame him. Although it easily could have been him at the helm. Scary shit, and lucky as the heavens...

Now that I refuse to take the helm, I am reading and eating some more. Trying to console my freaky nerves. Jesus, I'm glad this boat is built well!

11/20/00
North Carolina Coast

Somewhere north of Charleston, NC and it's about 45 degrees out. Holy fucking brrrrr! I'm wearing my polypro's under my jeans and two layers of fleece. So much for summer... Yesterday it was rainy and windy too, so we stayed anchored to sit out the crappy weather. Little did we know, but there is no end in sight. Today is Monday, and the forecast is for more cold and rain until at least Friday. Wonderful. I'm trying to remain cheery. And, of course, all I keep doing is eating. I woke up this morning and was thinking about Jim, Mexico, and the Sea of Cortez. I'm seriously considering the original plan of Mexico. It should only be a few more weeks until his current tugboat job is up, and then he should be looking at another few months off. I don't know... Matt and I have been having a good time, but he has this woman he's been seeing, and I think I may be out of a spot on the boat soon. I don't think they want a third wheel along! It's completely understandable. I guess she has a boat too, but it's currently broken down in Charleston. So that's where we're headed. To see if we can help her out.

On the brighter side of things, I've seen dolphins every day so far! They swim right up to the side of the boat. All shimmering and smiles, tilting their heads so that they can have eye contact with us. They're so cool! And pelicans everywhere. A few bald eagles, too. It feels humbling just to be a part of it all. The animal kingdom doesn't care how much peanut butter I intake. Being close to nature always fills my soul and makes me feel boundless gratitude for unjudged connection. Thanks, Universe!

I'm listening to Paula Cole at the moment and thinking of Josh. I hope he's doing well up there in the cold Alaskan darkness. Being in close quarters with another person who I don't connect with on anything but a surface level is really making me miss my connection to something comfortable and stable, like Josh and our Alaskan cabin. Thoughts of Josh bring me a feeling of solace while being alone in this new, foreign world of sailing.

11/21/00
Charleston NC

We arrived in the Charleston area yesterday afternoon and met up with Leslie (Matt's little blondie). He helped her fix her boat, and we went out to dinner together. Those two are like love-struck teenagers. They were staring into each other's eyes all night long. I'm kind of happy for him. I think this is what he was hoping for all along. Although it may be a very surface way to see things, they fit together in a physical sense. Both blond with blue eyes. She's short and thin, he's tall and thin. And both have not so perfect teeth. But now I'm finding myself searching for another boat to board once again. Matt decided that once in Florida, he's going to stay wherever Leslie stays. So much for the islands...

Enter Ron... The only guy I know in the anchorage with us right now. He's a single-handed guy from Canada on his way south and is open to having company on board. We're going to spend the day together today and see if we get along well enough to live on a boat with each other for a while. And, I'm finding that it's a mighty tall order to ask some sailor (they seem to all be men) to teach me some sailing skills, and not want to give anything sexual in return. It's one big continuation of male/female roles on land, unfortunately. Not that I'm closed off to a great relationship, or even a mutual fling. But I'm not getting into something sexual with someone specifically because they could see it as "payment." It's gotta be a connection of the right sort for that to happen for me.

This morning I was laying in my bunk trying to decide what I'm looking for, and I couldn't come up with anything except for Jim. But there are a lot of reservations there. That situation could definitely offer me a bit more than just a sailing buddy, but I'm not sure how deep I want to dive into that pool. The funny thing is that, presently, I really don't care. I'm like a feather floating in the wind. Sometimes I land in a place and stay for a while and then, when the wind picks up, I'm off flying around again. It's not necessarily a bad thing. Simply my current phase.

Well, next up is Ron. We'll see how that goes.

Thanksgiving Day 2000
North Carolina

Today finds me on yet another boat. This time with a woman. Completely safe and comfortable, with no expectations and mutual camaraderie. It's Leslie's 44-footer (yes, Matt's little blondie!). Yesterday I spent most of the day with Ron, and it all seemed to go okay. Not great, but okay. So, midafternoon I packed up my stuff and moved from Matt's boat to Ron's boat. Within a matter of an hour, I knew it was all wrong. He had just bought a TV, and it was right in the middle of the cabin where I was supposed to be sleeping. Bad sign. Then I realized he hadn't even started to clean out my berth, and it didn't look like he had any intention of doing so. Which left me with one place left to sleep—in the V berth with him. I tried to bring up the subject while unloading the grocery bags of provisions. At which time I end up pulling a newly bought porn video from the bag. Nope. That wasn't the deal. So I got on the VHF radio and put out an open call for help. It's always essential to know which VHF channels are the open stations in every port! As a fellow female solo sailor, Leslie came to my rescue. She immediately understood what was going on, and I once again moved all of my stuff onto yet another boat. Thank the goddess for good-hearted people!

Even though it's kind of crowded in here, given the 2 dogs, 3 cats, and 2 women, we have been talking all day and getting along swimmingly. And she didn't really seem to think I would impede her and Matt's jaunt down the ICW to their Florida destination. So, here I stay until there...

I've been trying to get in touch with Jim, too, wherever he is in between Columbia and Texas right now. My VHF capacity doesn't quite stretch as far as South America, but good old email works for us when his tugboat is in a port close enough for reception. It'll be good to hear his voice again and ponder some optional sailing possibilities.

Happy Turkey Day (says the vegetarian).

11/23/00
Beaufort, South Carolina

Spent the entire day wandering around Beaufort, SC in the rain. It was a downpour for most of the morning, and I highly enjoyed walking around getting drenched and jumping in puddles. Warm rain is such a new concept after years in Alaska! Although the wind picked up, it was in the 60s today. Can't imagine the oddity I must have looked like, all covered up in wet sailor's gear and jumping in puddles all over town! I couldn't have cared less! I was really happy to be off the boat and moving around a bit. Range of mobility is miniscule on a sailboat.

Checked out another option today. There is a woman anchored nearby whose husband had to leave to go back to work for a while, and now she's singlehanded and looking for a female crewmate. Leslie, Matt, and I met her yesterday at a pub in town while having lunch, and she seemed nice enough, but I have decided to stay with Leslie for a bit longer. It's been a nice change of pace to have a girlfriend I can talk with, and I think she feels the same way. But poor Matt, he lost his crew and now he's about to lose a girlfriend. It doesn't seem that Leslie is as into this whole thing as Matt. Unfortunate, but pretty common. Maybe I'll be able to get my crew spot back on his boat if he heads on to the Bahamas. Ah, the eternal opportunist, my new name... Tomorrow it's off to Savannah, GA, on to another state.

11/29/00 (I have no idea)
Savannah, Georgia

Leslie and I dropped anchor about two hours after a very
short motor to our new home for two days. Somewhere
off the Savannah coast. There is a soft, semi-warm breeze
blowing through my freshly washed hair. I even got hot
water to shower with today, and the sun was shining
through the open porthole to brighten my showering
experience. Warmer days are definitely welcome around
here! The sun has been blessing us with its warmth all
day and continues to beam its rays onto the
companionway, which is where I am presently standing.
Pelicans are flying overhead, and dolphins are playing in
the waves nearby. Since we have anchored, there have
been three other boats join us, and one of them is Matt's.
The tunes of Midnight Oil are being enjoyed on the deck
of Matt's boat, and I am grateful for the music coming
downwind. We have Leslie's comforter and bedding
spread out on deck to get aired out by the fresh breeze
and to dry off. After a day of heavy rains further north the
other day, it's necessary! My petting of the dogs is
creating a soft, steady wave of dog hair hovering over the
surface of the inlet. I suddenly have the feeling that this is
it. What it's all about. Enjoying the simplicity of life. No
expectations, the unknown of what tomorrow may or may
not bring, the simple freedom that comes with just being.
Blissfully enjoying the serenity of nothing and everything
all at once. Not thinking about yesterday or worrying
about tomorrow. Watching the freshly shed dog hair
softly blowing just above the smooth surface of the water,
past another anchored boat, and into the wispy, brown
reeds beyond, and finally mingling with the cottony

cattail seeds to disappear into the world at large... It's almost magical in its simplicity, yet utterly soul filling. This moment.

12/2/00
St. Simons Island, GA

This is now our third day here, and I am sitting in the cockpit listening to the beautiful, soothing sounds of profanity coming from the bilge. As we came into the anchorage here, right in front of a bridge, a 6-ft-tall bridge, the transmission went out. We were under motor, not sail, as usual, and it was NOT a good situation! In a frenzied panic, both Leslie and I dropped the anchor and prayed for it to hold. Being the newbie to this whole sailing thing, my reaction time to an imminent catastrophic situation was not ideal, to say the least...

We're motoring straight for the bridge to find a good anchorage, when the transmission gives out. There we are, headed straight for the bridge with only one possible way of stopping the boat from being crunched into the side of the concrete bridge pillars–the anchor. Leslie frantically and loudly yells at me to drop the anchor, which is my normal job, anyway. I go about my business of carefully lowering the chain a bit at a time to make sure the anchor gets a good grip on the bottom and doesn't drag. At which time, Leslie comes racing to the front of the boat and grabs the chain out of my hand to let it drop as quickly as possible to the canal floor. We both wait for the anchor to hold while watching the quickly approaching concrete pillars of the bridge get closer and closer with each second. The thought of what would happen if that anchor didn't hold was terrifying! We must have done something to appease the Gods. The anchor held!

And has held now for 3 days, because of the tide and the winds being on our side. Instead of worrying about the tranny on the first night, we went out and got drunk. It was all a bit too much to deal with and a great opportunity to forget about the current situation, I guess. We met our neighbor, Jon the painter, at the bar. His boat has been anchored here for close to a year, and he plans on heading down to Key West in a month or less. We also met a couple, Alex and Sherri, and ate about 15 pounds of oysters with them throughout the night. The margaritas were excellent, the oysters fresh and steamed, and the conversation stimulating. All in all, we had a much-needed break from the worries of the boat, if only for a few hours.

***

Given that we had no reason to rise and shine bright and early, we actually slept in until past 11 am! Inconceivable!! Such an enormous luxury, even if my head was pounding from those margaritas. The dogs were not thrilled to have to wait to take their morning dinghy ride to shore for their walk, but it's a dog's life sometimes. For the better part of the afternoon, Leslie poked and prodded and swore a bit until she figured out what was wrong with the tranny and we headed back into town to get the needed parts. A free lift into town from one of the shop owners at the marina was a pleasant and welcome surprise. People here have been helpful and very friendly. And Leslie is currently up to her elbows in grease and feeling much accomplished at her half-finished engine work. For an ex-stripper, soon to be high-end call girl, I would have to say that she does excellent mechanical work. Hopefully, we'll be out of this friendly but backwoods town either today or early tomorrow. On to safer anchorages and better margaritas...

12/9/00
St. Augustine, FL

Just ordered a margarita and a Caesar salad in a bar called A1A. It took some time, about a 6-mile walk to get here, but it is warm and beautiful! I'm actually wearing a sarong for the first time since this trip started—Yippee!! And I also found a two-piece bathing suit that won't kill underwater wildlife at the sight of me, which is a good thing, both for the wildlife and my ego. There is hope for the future, I guess...

***

So, there we were, sidling up to our first bar to enjoy a drink after our initial arrival in this town. Leslie and I. It was taking a while for the bartender to attend to us, when Leslie looks at me with this devilish smile and says,

"First one to get drinks bought for us gets the other one to buy us rain gear for the boat."

Seriously? I mean, this really isn't a very fair proposition considering she's a tiny, blonde-haired, blue-eyed cutie and I'm, well, I'm not. But I'm a risky entrepreneur and willing to take on this bet. Even knowing that Helly Hansen rain gear is going to set me back a few bucks.

"Game on," I answer with an equally devilish smile.

10 minutes later, I introduce Leslie to our new lesbian friends who would like to buy us a drink. I win! Oh, she was PISSED! Said I didn't play by the rules. Well, next time, make sure I know what the rules are, silly woman. The look on her face will have me laughing for years to come! I have a feeling I will be waiting a long time for my rain gear...

***

The newest activity in my life is a possible sail to Cuba. Very interesting, indeed... Leslie knows a South African guy sailing a 44-foot sloop that is headed to Cuba before the boat goes into dry dock. She's pretty sure he's looking for someone to crew for him. I'm waiting on a call from him to see what we might work out.

Leslie is now going by the alias of Anna. Her new job is driving a horse carriage around downtown. And Matt arrived yesterday. Poor guy thinks that we're going to be sailing together again, but I haven't mentioned the new Cuba possibility to him yet. We shall see...

St. Augustine seems like a very cool town, which is saying a lot for a Florida town. Their claim to fame is "the oldest town in the country" and its very European style. Lots of engraved lions and gargoyles and such in the bridge close to the anchorage and cool architecture. Admittedly, I have never been a big fan of Florida. But this has a different look and feel from the rest of Florida, and I'm enjoying that difference! It seems like there are more variations in demographics than just senior citizens here, as well, which is refreshing. Today I learned that there is actually a place in Florida that seems to not be a one-step-from-the-grave-population, strip mall heaven, same-as-every-other-place-in-the-state town. I am thankful!

12/10/00
St. Augustine, FL

Being on the boat with Leslie and having female companionship is such a welcome difference from being in male energy. Last night, while lying around onboard, we were working on our manifesting skills. Specifically, we were trying to conjure up a plate of loaded nachos out of thin air. Working in unison, we both focused on what the nachos would look like. An enormous pile of warm chips topped with melty, gooey cheese, black olives, diced tomatoes, jalapeno slices, black beans, salsa, and a nice heap of sour cream on top. And don't forget the avocado... Then we moved on to the aromas. The savory yet somewhat spicy smell of that delicious plate of nachos sitting in front of us. Unfortunately, our manifesting skills need a bit of fine tuning, because we spent quite a while trying to conjure up that beautiful, delicious plate of loaded nachos, to no avail. Finally, we had to give up the dream and give in to dreamtime, still longing for that crunchy, salty, savory sustenance.

Such is the life of a sailor. Being on a boat is not the instant gratification existence that is taken for granted so often by land dwellers. Sadly, I must get used to this...

Another difference about being on this particular boat is the presence of animals. Not just the sea life that I am growing to love, but dogs and cats. They're wonderful - full of unconditional love and acceptance. But having pets on a boat adds a bit more work and planning than being in a house with a grassy backyard. The cats, of course, have a litter box they use. No difference there. But the dogs need to go to shore every day. A few times, if possible. In the morning, Leslie's first order of necessity is to get all three of them loaded up in the dinghy and then take off to the closest shoreline. They get to romp around a bit and do their business. If there isn't an opportunity to take them ashore, they have a little patch of Astro turf, about 3 by 4 feet, on the back deck, for when nature calls. They're all trained very well to use their little patch of pseudo-nature, and it doesn't seem to bother them at all. Then we haul a bucket of sea water over the rail and wash it off. This little labor of love is totally worth the effort, though. Having pets around is so fulfilling to the soul! I so appreciate their love and hugs.

12/12/00
The Florida Keys!

Here I am, in the Florida Keys, so tacky and touristy. It's December, and I'm sweating my ass off with the sun beating down on me. Babes in bikinis, tanned he-men with their skimpily clad girlfriends, tourists with big beer bellies, hands occupied with cigarettes and daiquiris. And the time is high noon. Noelle and Tracy are my companions on this brief side excursion that we are taking for a week or so. The scene goes like this -

I'm in the boat's cockpit, on one of those rare days that we tied off at a slip instead of dropping anchor in the anchorage, when I hear a woman's voice calling my name.

"Lisa! Lisa! Is Lisa from Alaska here?"

I pop my head up to see my friend Noelle, from Alaska, walking up and down the docks, hollering for me, in St. Augustine. Wait, WHAT?! How is she here? And how did she know how to find me? I am utterly confused and bewildered, yet amazed and thankful for Noelle's ingenuity. The last time I saw her was when she was consoling me over lunch after I ripped apart the café down in Homer.

Turns out, one of her best friends lives in Florida, and she came down to visit. She had been following my adventures via email and knew I was on a boat in a marina in St. Augustine somewhere. So she came to find me. Super cool!! She and Tracy came and swept me off Leslie's boat for a quick side trip to the Keys before my sailing adventure continued on.

The cool, soothing sounds of Reggae playing in the distance, and the warmth of the sun on my body are a welcome enjoyment as I sit here in the Keys. The girls went to swim with dolphins today, and I couldn't get myself caught up with the tourist-trap indulgence. My current surroundings are daiquiri drinking, tan, fake-boobed, dyed blondes, and IQ-challenged college dudes. Seems like the only thing real around here are the palm trees, and I'm not 100% sure of that, either. I can see how, 20 years ago or so, this place must have been beautiful. But the almighty dollar has painted everything in rainbow colors, put a price tag on it, and doused it in expensive but necessary libations. But the ocean is 76 degrees and absolutely brilliant blue, and I have the next three hours to myself. I have spent the last three nights with Noelle and Tracy, and we're all having a great time bonding in our estrogen. We're headed down to Key West for the night and then taking a ferry to the Dry Tortugas to go camping. Before this trip, I wasn't even aware there was a place called the Dry Tortugas. My knowledge has expanded enough to know that they are the outermost islands in the Florida Keys. There's only a campground and a big fort on the last island. No residential or commercial crap allowed, which should be fantastic, considering most of the Keys have been infiltrated with neon signs for cheap hotels, cheesy trinket shops selling sand and shells, and dolphins enslaved for our swimming companionship. Along with the carnival of orange-colored humans...

I don't have my tent for this camping excursion, but I bought a tarp in case it rains, which I REALLY hope doesn't come to fruition! Then I have an entire week at my disposal before I go back up to St. Augustine, get on Richard's boat, and take off to Cuba.

(Oh, dear Lord, they're playing Lionel Richie... I'm definitely in cheesy music, neon sign, spring break heaven. HELP! Maybe I should have gone with the girls to see them swim with caged sea mammals. Patience and happiness, patience and happiness...)

Anyway, on another note, Richard... He's the South African guy Leslie set me up with for a trip to Cuba. He's coming south and should be in Florida in about ten days. Then we meet, get along wonderfully, and head to Cuba. That's the plan, at least. We've emailed a few times and talked a few times, and it seems okay so far. But, as I have learned well on this journey, you can't be sure of anything until it happens.

December something / 2000
Dry Tortugas, FL

We're here. We made it. Our merry trio of divine estrogen, in the Dry Tortugas... Slept under the stars and a full moon last night. It was quite windy, and I got little sleep, but it wasn't too bad. Last night was fun, though. And discovering this little paradise at the opposite end of the North American continent was definitely a wonder. $109 and 2 ½ hours was all it took to get here. The boat was more like a huge high-speed catamaran than a ferry, really. Ah, modern wonders of the sea... And now I have to put my tarp up so I don't get soaked when the imminently approaching rain comes down, which, unfortunately, is about to happen.

***

After having strategically hung my tarp between two palm trees to maximize rain coverage, I have returned to focus my attention to journaling. The guys in the next site, from Key Largo, are packing up and getting ready to catch the ferry back. One of them is a dive boat captain and windsurfed his way down here from Key Largo. That's about 170 miles and lots of open ocean. On a windsurfer! Now, this is a driven man. The other guy, his partner, makes his own beaded jewelry. We had a good chat this morning about our different processes of beading and our individual intricacies.

And then there's Annie. Another gypsy soul who is inhabiting this far-flung coastal key for the moment. She's called this place home for about a week so far and is valiantly trying to remain for as long as possible. Since there are no provisions here, no markets, cafés, or stores of any kind, she's been lightening the loads of other people when they leave the key—water, food, etc. Seems there is no shortage of leftovers! I haven't figured out what her story is as yet.

And Terri and his two friends... Terri is an outdoor education teacher. He comes down to the Keys a lot to teach kayaking. Don't know his friends yet.

Then there's the Fort. The Fort's claim to fame is that it's the biggest fort in the Americas. Being at the end of the Keys, at the tip of an island chain, it's obvious why there is a fort here. For visual positioning, obviously. But I haven't really gotten the specific history yet. The island is only about a mile wide, and the fort covers over ¾ of that space. Coral reefs inhabit the crystal-clear waters that surround this mile wide island and the snorkeling is quite nice! Lots of interesting sea creatures. Although I could have done without that toothy barracuda in my face. All shiny scales and razor teeth flashing around in front of me. That one was disconcerting. Luckily for me, his looks were pretty much the worst part of him.

Lots of palm trees and coral reefs. Not too shabby for a last-minute excursion with no planning or outdoor gear!

December 15, 2000
Dry Tortugas, FL

Every day brings with it the wonders of new people, places, and experiences. Yesterday afternoon, while browsing through the visitors' center of the Fort, I met

Jim. He and two friends had just dropped anchor, and after a brief chat, I learned he had been to Cuba, twice. So we sat and exchanged info for a while. It was fascinating to learn about what I'm getting into!

Got back to the girls about an hour later, and we all went for a snorkel, out beyond the mote wall. It never ceases to amaze me how much life is in the ocean. A whole other world down there that's just beyond our sight. Someday, I'm going to have to get my diving certificate.

Last night was one of those perfect nights that I find myself looking forward to now and then. An invitation onto Jim's boat with his friends offered me an evening of social comradery, along with rum and even a hot shower! There are really no words to describe the feeling of a hot shower after sleeping on a tarp in the sand and swimming in a salty ocean for a few days. I was so relaxed and appreciative, lounging on the settee, that it was an added indulgence that Jim was kind enough to offer me a back massage. That turned into a bit more than a back massage, which turned into a bit of a steamy and risqué encounter that left us both quite breathless. The ice in our rum and cokes was a much-appreciated luxury after that! It really was a perfect evening, watching the sun set behind an island surrounded by coral reefs with a cold drink in hand and stimulating conversation with new friends. And a bit of a seductively tantalizing encounter to top it off.

Once again, another one of those moments... This is what it's all about, the living life to its fullest thing. Simply enjoying these precious moments for what they are. No more, no less. No expectations, no judgements. Just being gratefully alive in the moment. BEING gratitude, love, and happiness.

Next Day

Another sunny, warm day on the island. Sitting in the hammock, still between two palm trees, with the sun rising at my back and the wind gusting through my hair. Noelle and Tracie departed on the Yankee Ferry yesterday. Travelling with those two, for that brief few days, was quite the trip! Tracie was a laugh a minute, quick with one-liners, but also a very closed person. At least to me, she was. Noelle's reaction to her energy was interesting, as well. From my perspective, the two of them were really quite inconsiderate of me. I'm not sure if it was just because they're besties, used to being alone in their own world, with me being a third wheel, or what. Not that I expected anything, but they didn't offer to share anything with me. I wasn't in need, specifically, but it made it awkward for me at times. For instance, we all came camping together. Actually, they asked me to join them. But I had no camping equipment. I left it all back in Phoenix stored in Jen and Mike's place because I didn't think I would need it. So, I bought a tarp to sleep under, and I figured I could use their cookstove. Once we got to the campsite, I had other campers offer me more helpful things than the girls did. People I had never met, offering whatever they could. They never offered for me to use their stove or put my pack in their tent when it rained. But I got coffee from the neighbor one morning and a ground cloth to sleep on from another neighbor. People were very sweet and giving. It was interesting to watch their behavior, considering another person joining their little party. Not upsetting, just interesting. I stayed here when their time was up, and I haven't been put out at all without them or any of their stuff. Oh well, I hope they enjoyed themselves. Some socialization with girlfriends is always a good time for me!

Last night I spent the better part of two hours bonding with a coconut. If you've ever tried to open a coconut with a Leatherman, you may know why some say it is impossible. It is not. But it definitely took a lot of patience, time, and work on my part! Everyone on the island told me I was wasting my time. While I was basking in the glory of my fresh, warm coconut milk straight from the nut, I took great pleasure in proving them wrong! Shit, that tasted delicious!

After my coconut experience, I went visiting with Terri and his friends. Their generosity afforded us a shared lobster dinner around the campfire. Fresh caught in the reefs outside of the mote of the Fort, by their own capable lobstering hands, no less. More appreciation for newfound friends on this island of sand. It was a delicious and fun evening!

I'm trying hard not to be too concerned about the excess 20 pounds that have taken residence on my body in the last four months. Jesus, this is getting out of hand.

My other camping neighbor, Annie, was kind enough to offer me a warm shower from her Sun Shower today. She's a hoot, this woman. An older woman in years, but definitely not old in spirit! The rest of the campers tried not to notice when she had no qualms about peeling her clothes off this afternoon and partaking of a warm shower from her little water bag hanging in the sunshine. It gave me a giggle. Good for her! I, being a bit more modest, kept my swimsuit on during my warm shower. Truth be told, I'm just a tad more than self-conscious about my ever-extending body! My prudish ways were more because of my insecurities than for the discomfort of any bystander.

When asked what Annie did for a living and how she could take the time to languidly vacation on this faraway island for any length of time, she only said she was a writer. I asked her what she had written, to which her response was something I had never read or heard of. Although, I am admittedly not much of a bookworm these days. I think she said something like "Pilgrim at Tinker Creek," to which she added was a long time ago. It must have been big in order to keep her financially stable currently. Not that she's spending money on a five-star hotel! But still... I appreciated my time with Annie. She's a really cool lady, and I aspire to be like her in my older years. Carefree and blithe...

(I didn't realize until years later that Annie Dillard had won a Pulitzer Prize for her book, "Pilgrim at Tinker Creek"!! Written a book... Ha! Pretty humble, aren't you, Annie?)

12/17/00
Key West, FL

Back to Key West today. Once again sleeping in the hostel here, in this intoxicated, neon-painted town. My stint on Leslie's boat has ended. She is outfitting her boat to leave the safety of the ICW and go out into open water. I'm sure the pets, alone, will be a feat to figure out, besides making sure the sails are up to par and the cabin is on lockdown enough that nothing flies around with the motion of the seas. And I, moving along to Richard's boat and heading for Cuba. My time spent with Leslie was a wonderful period of feminine bonding. I will miss being her "anchor bitch," being in charge of dropping and pulling anchor at every anchorage. And motoring the ICW was an experience. Learning the rules of busy traffic areas near ocean and river inlets. Radioing ahead for drawbridges. Sometimes waiting hours for drawbridges to open. Once in Florida waters, being aware and watching out for manatees, those slow, huge, beautiful water beings. I especially am thankful for getting to spend time on a female captained boat. Learning from another strong, independent, somewhat lunatic woman who has chosen this rarely–for our gender–trodden path. It was a wonderful chunk of time, and I am grateful. I wish her and her furry companions well on their open water adventures.

***

The boat ride back from the farthest of the Dry Tortugas islands was really rough, about six-to-eight-foot seas, but surprisingly, I didn't even feel the slightest bit seasick. My newly met ferry-sharing friends and I had the pleasure of enjoying a few margaritas together on our return voyage. Bob and Ernest are in their 70s and coming back from a four-day fishing trip off the tip of the Keys. They were splendid company on the hour-plus ride back! It didn't hurt that they picked up the bill, either. Thanks, guys!

My last two days on the island were beyond highly enjoyable! Opening coconuts with my Leatherman and then enjoying the warm, fresh coconut milk in my hammock under the palm trees with an incredible view of the sparkling blue ocean nearby. Partaking of a highly illegal, yet utterly delicious, freshly caught lobster with the kayak neighbors. Drinking rum and cokes aboard the

"Annie Victoria" at sunset with my three sailing friends while getting tips on Cuba for my upcoming trip. Oh, and the slight fling didn't really hinder the experience, either. Jim wanted to take me away from the world and sail off into the horizon together. Sure, Jim, whatever... Thanks for the experience, though! And that hot shower was much appreciated!

Such utter gratitude for a wonderful life... With unlimited thanks to the Universe for giving me the balls to grab these opportunities and turn them into exceptional experiences!

It always amazes me when I meet people who are so worried about me, as a single female, traveling alone. Would they worry if I were a male, I wonder? How strange, these borders we build for specific genders. Like being female is a detriment to the solo traveler. Oh, contraire! First, I am rarely "solo" with all the new friends I meet along the way. Second, being a single female traveler definitely has its advantages. Manifesting is one of my assets (besides nachos, that is), but when my own energies can't get me through a situation, I can always play the oh-I'm-just-a-helpless-solo-female-please-help-me card. Don't get me wrong, that card is played only when ABSOLUTELY NECESSARY! Try getting away with that shit as a single male traveler—NOT! Just sayin'...

My first day back to Key West, I also received an email from Richard. He'll be in St. Augustine in two days. Looks like I'm headed back up that way to go meet up with him and hopefully start a Cuban adventure.

Right now, I'm focused on creating positivity. Create, create, create... And then believe in achieving those amazingly adventurous goals!

Around Xmas 2000
Ft. Lauderdale coast

My first time putting up the sail today. And I have to admit, it was hellish! Richard and I had just motored out past the jetty in Ft. Lauderdale. A heavy drizzle fell from gray clouds. Not quite crazy windy, but enough to scare me into having a quickened pulse. It was my first time on open water, and I had much apprehension. But I had signed on to this adventure, so no backing down now... Richard looked at me and, hollering over the wind, told me to go set a reef in the sail. Thinking I know what he means, I scamper up to the foredeck and am promptly filled with utter panic. Water is pelting me from every direction. The spray from the bow hitting the waves head-on is slowly drenching me with salt water, and the steady pelting of rain is simultaneously rinsing off the salty spray. Water is the least of my problems at the moment, unfortunately. As I strain to hear the instructions being screamed to me through the cacophony of rain and waves, along with a howling wind, the fear of messing this task up is terrifying me. Okay, focus... Tune out the wind, the waves, and the rain. Try to get a good foothold. Sway with the motion and not against it. Eye contact with Richard, the captain of this vessel. Now, what is he yelling? For the love of God, I can't hear through all of this chaos! His lips are moving. I can see that much through the blinding rain and my own tears of frustration. Or maybe it's the over-exuberant pounding of my heart because of my rising level of fear that is deafening me. Focus!! Okay, something about lines and the mast... Hoisting, pulling, folding of the sail... Then another few repetitive motions of tying down the lines. Oh... No... Don't lose my foothold! No slipping now! Hold on, that was an enormous wave. Wipe the saltwater out of my eyes and come back into focus on the task at hand. Just get a reef set in this uncompromising sail, and then I can get back into the relative safety of the cockpit.

Soaking wet, but beyond frustration to a sort of giddy sense of accomplishment, I wobble and slip my way back to the cockpit with a huge grin on my face, despite the lines of salty tears from minutes before. Unbelievably, I accomplished the mission at hand. My sailing adventure has begun!

Now I sit in my berth. All cozy and tucked in. Safe at anchor. My wet gear at the foot of my bunk. And wonder how the hell I get myself into these situations?!

So far, Richard and I are getting along okay. Not exactly besties, but cordial and respectful towards each other. I wonder how a few months on this boat is going to be with just the two of us. He definitely seems to grasp the whole captain thing; he's knowledgeable, at least. There's no chemistry there at all, which is nice. One less drama to worry about. I'm not looking for a romance. I only want to learn how to sail. Oh, and the prospect of seeing Cuba is exciting too! Especially since it's basically illegal for me to go there.

12/23/00
West Palm Beach, FL

It's a joy to be eating once again! After two days of hanging over the stern rail turning green and puking my guts up, Richard and I, well, actually just Richard, stopped about eight hours early in West Palm Beach instead of going the distance to Ft. Lauderdale. Winds picked up to almost 30 knots and seas were about six to eight feet (possibly more) for my first trip out to open ocean. Hence, the hanging over the stern rail for most of the time. I'm going to have to toughen my innards up before we actually head across the Straight for Cuba, or I'm in big trouble.

Even though it was not a pleasant experience at all to be puking my guts up, I didn't let it get to me too much because I was actually SAILING!! Finally! We left St. Augustine, and the people there, yesterday morning at about 7:30 am and spent the last two days taking turns at the helm in three-hour shifts in seas that seemed to wrench my guts out with merciless fury. I think next time I'll take some Dramamine with me. Stupid, stupid, stupid woman... But I got to sail, and it's really warm here now. So it's all good!

Cold weather – poor visibility – wind having a hard time filling the sails – seas getting bigger- wind blowing harder – not a soul in sight for days – sleeping in 3-hour increments – if you can find sleep while crashing around in 8-foot swells slamming everything in the cabin back and forth – here and there. Puking over the rails while at the helm for days, praying for a settled stomach – and then the dolphins show up playing at the bow – stars are shooting above your head in the night sky – the anchor drops, and somehow you only remember how utterly amazing it is – this sailing thing – it's all worth it.

Tomorrow we return to the relentless, awaiting sea.

Xmas Day, 2000
Where the Hell am I?

Christmas Day, what does it mean, anyway? A huge
commercial endeavor solely focused on gaining profits.
I'm lonely. I miss Deb, Josh, the rest of the family, my
friends, and Boomer. What the fuck am I doing? I'm
having one of those moments where I'm questioning my
sanity. I have no safety net, no comfort zone, no close
friends here, and am feeling really down. Holidays are
hard when you're single. But in my situation, they're even
harder right now.

Tonight, I called Cindy's house to speak with Deb,
and everyone was there but me. For the first time in 10
years, the entire family was together, and I was the only
one missing. Got off the phone and cried. After a good cry
and a bit of feeling extremely sorry for myself, I pulled
myself together and realized how good it is to be me, and
I'm back on track again. Richard and I are going out to
dinner tonight, and Elizabeth arrives tomorrow. He just
met her at a bar the other night, and they hit it off, so I
guess she's going to come visit the boat now and see his
world a bit more. New Year will be much better, I'm sure.

12/29/00
Key West

Dolphins. Five of them were playing in the water by the
boat today. That's one of the great things about anchoring
out instead of getting a slip at the dock. It's closer to all
the things that matter. The dolphins are wonderful,

radiant creatures that, I am more than certain, understand human emotional needs. They always show up at precisely the right moment. And they always bring a smile to my face, no matter what. They are highly loveable creatures, and I am entrapped by their happy spell.

We're still in Key West awaiting a good weather window to take off to Cuba. I'm understanding that, in the sailing world, the sailor spends way more time waiting for weather windows than actually sailing.

Somewhere around New Year 2000/2001 Key West, FL

Unfreakingbelievable! She's coming to Cuba.

"Oh, by the way, we're stopping to pick up Elizabeth on the way to the store. She's coming with us," he says nonchalantly. Coming with us? Huh? Where? To the store?

As simple as that. So, on our way to our last provisions expedition, we stopped and picked her up, and she is now part of the crew. We set sail this morning. All three of us. A happy little unit, or so I'm praying. Myself, Richard, the South African Captain, and Elizabeth, the woman he met in the bar a few nights ago. And this is the beginning of our sail to Cuba from Ft. Lauderdale. We're all thinking we could be "under sail" for up to 2 months. I'm a bit torn about this new turn of events with a third person on board. It could be great for me, seeing as how Richard and I get along well enough, but we are not by any means the best of friends. Elizabeth could be exactly the energy needed to appease the slight discomfort between us. But if Elizabeth and I don't get along, this whole thing could be disastrous. I guess I'm about to find out!

Most of my adult life could be considered unconventional, and my current situation promises no less of an adventure. Currently, I have just set sail to an island that is illegal for me to visit, with people I hardly know, on a boat I have no idea how to sail.

Sure! Why not?

But seriously, even with the questionable addition of an unknown third person added to an already questionable mix, I'm excited about this adventure! I guess I owe thanks to Leslie. If it weren't for her, I wouldn't have met Richard and would not be on this boat heading to Cuba. At least it's promising to not be boring!

December 30, 2000
Still Key West

I wanted to read a book tonight but can't go back into the main cabin because Richard and Elizabeth are obviously making up for a few days of lost time. The not so soft moans and groans are my clue to stay the hell away. I'm realizing my luck in having a back berth just beyond a center cockpit right about now. So here it is, 9:10pm the night before New Year's Eve, and I've been drinking most of the day in Key West. Those toxic-colored slushy drinks can really pack a punch! I don't even want to know what makes them that color. TMI...

I've also been searching for ATMs that have any $$ in them to spit out at me. Possibly leaving for Cuba tomorrow, all depending on the weather. Eating, drinking, and yes, smoking way too much and not really caring because of the amount of attention I seem to get from the opposite sex. Obviously, I've still got some kind of appeal, despite my rising weight level, because I keep having to turn them down. Even the fact that I haven't showered in days doesn't seem to deter them. I'm sure the constant state of inebriation that everyone seems to be in around here doesn't hurt my appeal, either. Honestly, I'm not interested in any of them. It feels fantastic to not want any of them, too. Sometimes it serves me well to take a break from that whole pheromonal thing. I mean, really, let it go. Get a grip. Feel the single-ness for a while. It's okay.

I've been drowning any emotions that I may have in booze and cigarettes for the past couple of days, and it seems to be working fine! I will now contemplate the level of my happiness while I go to sleep listening to the sound of the water lightly slapping against the hull of the boat at anchor. Sweet dreams for now...

Jan 6, 2001
Bahia Honda, Cuba

Slept half the night on deck last night, but the wind started up, so I ended up in my little back berth condo by the end of the night. Had a few very realistic dreams. I guess you could call them lucid. The most prominent one being about Steve in Alaska. I was sitting next to him on a barstool or something similar, his hair was pulled back like it normally is, and I was telling him how much I loved him. We were both smiling and laughing, and it felt great. That's it. That's all I can remember about it. But I woke up having to pee really bad, and I felt like a truck had hit me.

Not really sure what the significance of that dream was. Pretty sure it had nothing to do with Steve, but more to do with being comfortable back in Alaska again.

***

Presently, I am sitting on deck in the sunshine in a place called Bahia Honda on the northwest coast of Cuba. It's flat calm, which is the first I've seen of this beautiful, windless weather.

The sun is shining; it is warm, and I could easily describe the scenery as spectacular. We are the only boat anchored in this enormous bay overlooking the distant mountains, and it was a blessing to have the local catch of red snapper for last night's dinner. There is a beautiful sandy beach off the bow of the boat and fucking COLD water! Besides the water, this is about as close to perfect as it gets. And I'm hoping that it will only get better. My psyche hasn't been in the best state, however, and I'm trying to sort that out. Since it's been a while since I've gotten in touch with anything spiritual, maybe communing with my animal spirits will help. I'm going to pull some medicine cards and see what words of wisdom they may have for me.

1/9/01
Santa Lucia, Cuba

Had more dreams about Steve last night. I'm not sure if they were actually about him, but definitely about Alaska, once again. It's funny how Steve is coming up in my

71

subconscious. Why him? It's not like we were really serious or long term. Way better friends than anything else. It's possible that he represents the male part of myself in my dreamworld. I haven't figured it out. I think the Alaska part of the dreams is simply because I have been thinking a lot lately of what I'm going to do after this time in Cuba. Mostly my conscious, daytime thoughts are of heading back to Colorado for a while. Hiking and snowboarding, hanging out with Deb and Donna, seeing Jen and all the old crew, and priority is losing this excess weight I seem to have collected. I always lose the weight when I go back to Colorado, so that's good. Then there's Jim in Mexico, still a possibility. That would be good too, but it's stepping back. And I'm all too aware of what happens when you try to regain something that wasn't there in the first place. And yet, still, my subconscious keeps giving me dreams of Alaska and the people that I have come to know up there. Shannon and Jonathan, now known as Shanothan to me, have also been on my mind recently.

But for the moment, here I am. In Cuba. I need to enjoy what is in front of me at the time it's in front of me. I created this for myself, so why is it so hard sometimes to focus on the NOW? But we definitely are having a good time, so SHIFT my focus on here. Be. Here. Now.

Later that day

Where to start? The people of Santa Lucia are wonderfully happy, friendly people. Upon our first walk through town, a local named George (hor-hay) befriended us and showed us everything and anything we wanted to see. Not only did he walk us around and show us all the stores and schools, etc., but he went well out of his way to get us anything we needed. He had other locals climbing trees to fetch us coconuts, found us oranges and wine and rum and garlic and more coconuts. We had beer at the "Casa Particular," a home that offers various services to the locals (no, not THOSE kinds of services!). There were women in the kitchen painting each other's fingernails. Interesting... We found a casa that sold us freshly made helado, ice cream. That was quite the adventure.

We were all walking down the little dirt street in town when we passed a local eating what looked like an ice cream popsicle. It looked mouthwateringly delicious, and we asked where we could get some. He pointed down the road to a little adobe hacienda. Off we went to find the helado. Upon arriving at the hacienda, we knocked on the door, and a semi-stooped over older Cuban woman answered. We did the best we could in our broken Spanish to explain that we were sent to get ice cream here at this house.

"Si, si, si!" she said excitedly, while gesturing us through the tattered wooden door. Much to our surprise, she ushered us through the house. Into the sitting room, where there was an old man on a rickety chair. Then through the bedroom which had a freshly made bed sitting vacant for the moment, and finally into the kitchen where the woman opened up the freezer part of her cold box and took out a few freshly made helado popsicles. We offered her a few Cuban coins, which she accepted, and then proceeded back through the hacienda and out the front door again. Once out on the street, with sticky, creamy streaks on our faces, we all lapped up the best ice cream we had ever had the pleasure of savoring! Oy, dios mio!! If ice cream could be orgasmic, this was such ice cream. Really, the best any of us had ever had.

After the ice cream experience, we went to George's casa to fetch an empty bottle so we could get rum from the local pub. We didn't know it, but in order to get rum here, you have to bring them a bottle. They then fill it from a big wooden barrel with a tap on it, straight into your bottle. So cool! It was wonderful to feel so welcomed and well received in this little communist town on the Cuban coast, by people who have so little and will happily share every bit of it! Pigs, chickens, goats, dogs, horses, and other various things wandering about in the streets and yards in search of a scrap to nibble upon.

The best part was that George didn't really want anything for his time or efforts. In my experience, when a local in a foreign country takes you on for the day, there is always a fee expected for these niceties. They get so few tourists here, and so few opportunities to talk to anyone from outside of Cuba, that George was just happy to be showing us his beautiful country and introducing us to his people. As well as getting to chat with some exotic strangers for the day. It was an amazing experience! And I'm sure he'll be the talk among his comrades for a while to come. Basically, we upped his street cred exponentially!

And tonight, the three of us and the couple from the other boat docked here–Steve and Judy on Dos Tintos- will join George and Jeremy, their Cuban guide for the day, for a fish dinner cooked Cuban style. How utterly wonderful!

And then there was the market. We jumped on the opportunity to go visit an open market today, kind of like a farmers' market to us in the States. So many smells and colors! But I learned a very humbling lesson today at market. I believe all three of us were humbled. Our upper-class privilege was uncomfortably, and palpably, handed to us without an invitation, but also innocently and without malice.

We went to the Panaria (bakery) to buy bread, and when we asked "cuanto questa?" (how much) we were told, in very broken English and lots of hand motions, that without a "ticket" the baker could not give us bread. It was not for sale. We were told to come back at the end of the day, and if there was bread left, THEN he could take some money for it and we could have the bread. But before then, no bread for us. We were all very confused and not really sure what was going on. I mean, so far, these people had been nothing but open and giving, and now we're being told no to buying bread.

Basically, Cuba has not had an open monetary system for a long time. No money. Until about two years previously, when the government opened up the financial market to a 20% allowable income via money at the local markets. The way their socialist system works is that everyone in a village had means to give back to the village. Some people were fisherman and brought fish to market, others made rope and brought rope to market, others harvested fruits and vegetable, others eggs and meat, etc. All of these village members got "tickets" in return for what they offered to their village. They then traded these tickets at market for other goods. For instance, you're a villager and go to market and use your tickets to "pay" for other goods you might need. It's like a barter system. Almost like what our money used to be. Since we didn't have any tickets, as such, we had offered nothing to their community. The baker wouldn't give us bread until he knew that all the villagers had their needs met. Then, at the end of the day, if there was bread leftover, he could take some money from us for trade for the bread. But only up to 20% of his product, as per government regulations. In this way, the villagers knew they would have their basic necessities without having the need for money. And then they could make a bit extra on the "open market," so to speak.

It was a very humbling moment for me, and I felt like an asshole, honestly, to assume that my piece of paper was good enough to take bread from people that need it. That's how I interpreted the situation. I felt very white, very privileged, very humbled, and quite embarrassed. And it really got my mind going as to how capitalism works. More so, how it doesn't work.

Very interesting, what traveling does to illuminate other ways of being. Very interesting, indeed.

Jan 10, 2001
Grande Rapado, Cuba

Tonight, we are anchored in a place called Grande Rapado, illegally, because there are no guarda here to search the boat. What a beautiful change from all our stops in Cuba so far! A night of peace and quiet in a deserted anchorage with our fellow travelers, Dos Tintos, with no guarda to search the boat and exchange lots of meaningless paperwork! Yippee! Under a full moon, no less.

***

Last night was excellent. The three of us, including Judy and Steve from Dos Tintos, went into San Lucia at 8 pm to meet up with our hosts, Jeremy and George. We bought the beer (at 75 cents each, which was crazy amounts of money to them and really miniscule to us!), and they had dinner ready. A ten-pound snapper was grilled and beautifully displayed on a platter with sliced cabbage and orange sections. As it turned out, they had managed to open the only discotheque in town specifically for our festive dinner party. Open air and food and music were shared by the five of us cruisers and about six of their Cuban friends. We danced, ate, and had a good time until about midnight. After talking to our hosts throughout the night, we discovered that only about 15 boats stop in this quaint little town throughout the span of a year. Little did we know that these locals of Santa Lucia had gone well out of their way to throw us this party, since they get so few opportunities to meet foreign travelers. I felt extremely fortunate to be at the receiving end of all their sincere hospitality! All of us had a wonderful time and greatly appreciated their efforts to make us feel so welcome.

It was a bit surprising to find out the reason Jeremy and George kept intermittently disappearing out the front gate. Seems that they had concerns about the Guarda finding out about our little party. Little did we know, but if they had been found out, they would have been in a pickle over the festivities. The Guarda don't take kindly to the locals hanging out with the touristas. Seems they are afraid of locals trying to stow-away on boats and escaping, which is pretty much the only reason for our checking in and out of every anchorage and dock we stop at. The Guarda comes onboard, with guns and ammo slung over their shoulders, to make sure we aren't helping anyone out of the country.

Every place has its thing... But it was definitely a night to remember. Lots of good people, fun, laughter, dancing... "the night of the dancing gustapo—mira, mira, Elizabeth...!" A great time!

Elizabeth and Lisa in Cuba 2001 "Kind of like a convulsion, only less controlled."

Jan 11, 2001
La Fe, Cuba

His name was Jonathan. Thirty-one years old, tall, blond, blue eyes, a great sense of humor, and his birthday was the beginning of July sometime. And I knew this without asking him. I just knew. It was one of those incidents where I didn't need to ask one question, I just had to look at him. He was "the one," and I knew it.

What a glorious dream! Of course, I know it exists; I simply have to be ready for it.

Of course, this sets my thoughts to Warren. Ah, Warren... The South African who I thought was the love of my life but then crushed me like an overripe grape. Warren and I met years ago when I was living in Colorado. Glenwood Springs, to be exact. I was bartending one night when he came in with a few friends and sat at a booth at the bar and ordered coffee all night long. Due to his curly, blond hair, blue eyes, and South African accent (I'm a complete sucker for accents!), I overlooked this obvious annoyance of him squatting at the table with very little chance of a tip after hours of coffee drinking. That night was the beginning of a tumultuous affair that lasted a few years. The end of which found me alone, after being dumped, in Cape Town, South Africa. He was the one. Or so I was convinced; and pretty much have been since then. My memories of him, more specifically the memories of my heart cracking wide open while traveling alone through a foreign country, have made me keep a "healthy" distance from true intimacy ever since. Actually, it's as far from healthy as it gets. I try not to think about him too often, or let my mind make up things that could never be. But after a dream like that, it's challenging to not go backwards... I'll simply relish this Jonathan character for the moment, thank you very much, and be extremely thankful that he didn't come to me as Warren in my dream!

Jan 13, 2001
South Coast of Cuba

Somewhere on the south coast of Cuba, and I've felt pretty shitty all day today. Feeling very fat and lonely. No emotional contact for quite a while. The day started out with rough seas and wind straight on the bow. Not exactly wonderful sailing conditions. But Richard actually let me sleep last night, instead of waking me for a helm shift. We pulled anchor at around midnight, and I had gone to sleep at about 8:30 with a splitting headache. He pulled anchor and set sail by himself last night and let Elizabeth and I sleep. I was extremely grateful when he didn't wake me for my watch until 5 am! Then, this afternoon, he was asleep on the settee and Elizabeth was passed out in the V Berth when the dolphins arrived. I haven't seen dolphins since leaving Key West, and when they showed up today, my mood turned around immediately. There were about 10 of them, splashing about and playing at the bow. It's like they inherently understand when I need their energy. They know how happy they make me. They can see me watching them, and they put on quite the show for me. I mean, eye to eye contact, with them swimming sideways in order to see me directly. And it was all for me. Everyone else was sleeping. Dolphins are amazing and wonderful beings! It was a completely soul filling experience!

***

Lately, I've been feeling really lonely and homesick for Alaska. I really miss Josh and the love we shared. It's strange how, when I have been by myself for a long time, I feel like I will never find that kind of intimacy again. And I long for it daily now. To have someone to talk to, to hold and touch, to open up to and be accepted. My quota of 8 hugs a day has been cut down to about one a week, and the effects are starting to show. I miss my friends, my cabin, Boomer, and driving around Homer and walking on the Spit. Watching the eagles and moose. But at the same time, trying to appreciate each moment as it happens. The dolphins showing up today in this crystal-clear water helped a lot. And my physical appearance, due to way too much food and an extreme lack of exercise, has taken its toll on me emotionally as well as physically. Tomorrow I will swim and walk on the beach of this seemingly perfect isolated tropical island off the south coast of mainland Cuba, and try to regain the happiness and patience I am striving to find.

Palm trees, coconuts, lobster, and dreams–Cuba 2001.

1/14/01
South Coast of Cuba

The energetics between the three of us have been a bit
tense at times. More specifically, between Richard and I.
Elizabeth and I have made a sort of silent pact to have
each other's backs. But Richard and I are like oil and
water sometimes. I'm not really sure if he's not happy
that I'm here, breaking into their little love tryst on a
sailing excursion around a beautiful island, or if he just
doesn't like me. It's not like anything blatant or rude, but
it's more like an underlying negative energy. Sometimes
he makes me feel like an unwanted stranger on his boat.
But he's kinda stuck in having to deal with me because we
made a deal, and he's going to stick to it. Also, I do a lot
more work on this boat than Elizabeth does, and I'm
pretty sure we're all aware of that. I'm not sleeping with
the captain, so it's required of me to do more labor, is
pretty much how it's working. Not that I hold that against
Elizabeth. I'm more than happy that she jumped on
board at the last second. She's the peacemaker between
Ricard and I. For instance, the other day Richard was
giving me a course mapping lesson. It was a beautiful
day, as we were sailing along the coast of the island. We
had the map opened up in the cockpit and a course set.
Richard disappeared below deck to grab something from
the galley when the depth finder started descending.
Rapidly. We were really close to the shoreline, but the
map showed that there was a sharp drop-off and we
should have been on a completely safe course. But that's
not what the depth finder was saying.

"Richard, get up here. We're losing depth fast, and I
don't know what to do!" I cried out, alarmed.

"You're okay. You got this. Just keep course. Look at the map," he responded from the galley.

The rocky coastline is getting closer at this point. The depth finder is getting lower.

"Richard! I'm not okay! Get up here!" I was now getting panicked.

Once again, a retort instead of actually coming to help, "C'mon, you wanted to learn. Figure it out. You can do it."

As I'm watching the slideshow in my mind of the boat crashing into the rocks along shore, "Fuck you. I'm off the wheel!" And I stormed to the back deck.

He finally came running up and realized, just in time, that we were indeed about to crash into the reef close to the shoreline. He quickly changed our course and then stopped talking to me for the better part of the day.

What the fuck, dude? It was my first time at mapping. I was uncomfortable. You left me high and dry. It's your fucking boat! And now you're pissed at ME???

Elizabeth stepped in after a bit and talked to him. He did offer me a half-assed apology after she made him. A 44-foot boat is not a great place to be stuck when energies don't merge. There's absolutely no way of escaping.

Jan 16, '01
Cayo Real, Cuba

Baking bread has become a kind of Zen meditation thing on the boat. We have no refrigeration, so we're living pretty minimalistic. Butter and cheese only last a few days in this humidity before going moldy, so it's been a lot of cabbage and dry goods. But we do have gas to run

the oven. And a lot of time to make bread. And so it is–
bread is a major staple on this boat. Elizabeth and I have
contests on who can make the best bread. Richard, of
course, is the judge, which doesn't really seem very fair to
me, but I have no other alternatives. Admittedly, both of
our bread is pretty fucking good. After mixing it all up
and kneading the dough, we let it sit out on deck for a few
hours in the sun. We went snorkeling the other day while
we let the dough rise and were greeted with quite the
surprise when we returned. The yeast loves the warm,
humid temps, and the dough joyously escaped from the
bowl and started to take over the cockpit. Like an oozing
blob in one of those old movies that always seems to take
over cities. But in a happy, delicious kind of way!

Today comprised of baking bread, eating crepes for
breakfast, basking in the sun naked, showering under the
perfectly clear blue skies in the cockpit, snorkeling,
swimming, walking on the beach, eating coconut while
playing in the sand, and the dinner feast. Richard caught
4 lobsters, and along with the conch I "harvested" earlier,
we had a fresh crustacean feast onboard! Absolute YUM!
Along with wine, Cuban cigars, and lots of stars shining
down upon our happy little trio, I shall begin my dreams
for this evening. I hope they can compare with my
current reality.

Gratitude and abundance.

Jan 17, 2001
Aboard Coquette Somewhere

This morning, I decided I would try to smooth out some
of the friction between us after the map coursing

incident, and got up early and made those guys coffee in bed. I got it all ready, just the way everyone likes it, and ceremoniously delivered it to the awaiting crew members, still in bed in the V-berth. Everyone was all happy and thankful until Richard took a sip and this wretched look took over his face. The coffee came out in a spit-like guffaw and a big, loud "ACKKKKKK!!!!!!! Are you trying to kill me?!" What the hell??

It turns out I used the leftover water that was in the pot already on the stovetop. Unbeknownst to me, it was sea water and not fresh water. And, as luck would have it, Richard was the first one to take a sip. Oops... HAAAA!!! I swear, I didn't do it on purpose! Of course, he doesn't believe me, and my kind actions did exactly the opposite of what I was intending. Seems that there's still some friction on the boat (said with a big sigh and eye roll). Although it was pretty damned funny–he he he...

Jan 18, 2001
Juventud (Isla de)

For some reason unknown to the three of us, the Guarda let us anchor out in the bay just south of the Guarda station. They told the three other cruiser boats they couldn't anchor there, and they had to pay to dock. Well, thanks, I guess...

Last night I spent most of the night running to the head and feeling quite shitty in general (pun intended). Believe it or not, we all think it was from too much lobster. Protein overload. What a way to go, huh? Tomorrow we actually get a day to do nothing. A day "on the hook," so to speak. Time for some beading, maybe. Or maybe just focus some good energy to my internal organs. I might go for a swim, but we're near a mangrove and the water is looking a bit brackish. Not quite the clear blue waters of some of our beach anchorages. But maybe...

Jan 21, 2001
South of Nueva Gerona

After spending the night in a towel on the settee, between many trips to the head, we all decided it was best if I went to the doctor in town today. Not that I'm keen on going to the doctor, but the prospect of sitting on the toilet for another night was not an appealing option! So, Richard quickly pulled anchor, and we motored around to the Guarda station so Elizabeth and I could catch the 8 am, one-hour bus ride to Nueva Gerona. We made it to the hospital–General Medicine office–and the doctor took us in immediately. I was a bit guilt-ridden about that fact, simply because he rushed us past a long line of waiting locals and into the exam room. He poked and prodded my stomach, asked a few questions, and then gave me a prescription to "kill the parasites." The exam room, or office actually, was no more than a small desk and a stainless-steel table. There was no door, just a hanging curtain. Nothing on the desk but a few tongue depressors and prescription forms. Then the assistant that was helping the doctor walked us down the street to the Pharmacia to fill the prescriptions. Antibiotics, 7 days' worth of two types of pills, good for 3 people, just in case it had spread to Elizabeth and Richard, cost the equivalent of 50 cents! No charge for the doctor's visit or the exam, just 50 cents for the prescription. For all of us. 50 cents.

Holy Mary, Mother of God... This ain't the good 'ol U S of A, that's for freakin' sure'!! And, statistically, Cuba has the lowest rate of illness in the world. And the entire system is compensated by the government. No charge at all. What a concept! Such a load of bullshit we're fed in America. What a completely EVIL thing socialism is... It seems better than putting a billion-dollar price tag on human life. It's infuriating. Oh, I could go on and on...

***

The bus ride into town was beautiful. Green lushness filled my senses from the interior of this tropical island and old-world culture. Chickens running around yards, children playing in the streets, people waving at us as we drove by as part of the local scene on the public bus. It's really a shame that our style of cruising is not really allowing us to experience much of what the culture of Cuba is about. We're staying mostly to the coast and more remote areas. Not that that's a terrible thing, just that I'm finding it's definitely not a consensus, our little sailing trio. Richard is slowly driving me batty. Considering that I have my preconceived notions of single South African men (that sordid episode with the love of my life who ditched me after flying 3000 miles to be with him a few years back may have negatively biased me just a little), maybe I'm being skewed in my view of things. There are days when I feel like I'm a prisoner on the boat and would do anything to get back to the States and off this floating jail. But really, I guess I shouldn't blame it all on him. Our travel styles are completely different. He is perfectly fine with sitting on the boat for days on end, or going for a swim now and then. My body and mind need to be more active. I desperately need to hike and miss the connection to my feet on the Earth immensely. The bus ride through the lush tropical inland was like a carrot on a string, dangling just in front of my face and then yanked backward just as I got within striking distance. Back onto the boat with me. Bottom line is that I'm lonely, am craving human contact in just about any way possible, and feel completely unvalidated, unwanted, and kind of boxed in at the same time. These two are like spring rabbits and are not so concerned about this third wheel. Just a few more weeks. I can do it!

But at least my bowels have tightened up and I'm not running to the head every 5 minutes. It's the small things... Well, actually, that's a pretty big thing!

End of Jan, 2001
South coast of Juventud (Isla de)

On our way to Cayo Mattias, we're anchored off right in the middle of the coast in the only possible anchorage. And it's absolutely perfect. White sandy beaches, clear blue water, a quaint little 60s style lighthouse, and more solitude. The three of us have our ups and downs, and this day is definitely an up. Went swimming naked as soon as the anchor went overboard and came back with a conch to add to our veggie stew. Set the sails and pulled anchor this morning with no motor. Very peaceful.

Later

Being stuck on a boat gives one plenty of time to ponder things. And since we are here in Cuba, I am pondering the Cuban existence. Everywhere we have gone in Cuba, the people are happy and welcoming. After traveling through numerous third world countries, this is a very unusual and welcome occurrence. Not that people in other countries haven't been happy or welcoming, to some extent, but here, it's different. These are the happiest people I've ever met. As an American, we have all been fed this image of how terrible Cuba is. How horrible communism is, and how the standard of life for these people is deplorable. Now that I'm here and experiencing this firsthand, I'm finding all of that to be a bunch of bullshit. Take George, for example, our previous "guide" a while back. He spent the entire day taking us under his wing, introducing us to his people, touring us through his town, helping us to get our provisioning needs met, and even throwing a party for us with a few of his friends and comrades in town. In my experience, I would usually get somewhat suspicious and nervous, thinking about what he might want in payment. There's ALWAYS some kind of payment expected, and usually it's a great way to scam unsuspecting tourists out of WAY too much money. But not here. Not with George. Or anyone else we've encountered here, for that matter. These people are genuinely happy to give. They are proud of their land and their people. And I believe that, due to the fact that few tourists come here, it's a rare and precious gift for them to get to know us. They want to hear about us as much as they want to show us their world. It's beyond refreshing and really quite heartwarming.

Don't get me wrong. I'm not saying they live in a Utopian society. There are still Guarda everywhere. Carrying their machine guns in open view and making sure the locals don't get too many ideas about "escaping." So, it's definitely not an ideal situation for the locals. But they do have everything they need. They get their needs met on a basic level. Their healthcare system sure as hell beats ours in the US.

What we learned by chatting with the miscellaneous locals here is this—for one, the older the local, the more history we get and the unhappier they are in Cuba. They are old enough to remember how it was before Castro and our embargo against them. They remember a Cuba without Guarda or machine guns constantly in sight. Their memory recalls the hard times they went through while the country was trying to figure out how to be self-sustained. On average, every Cuban citizen lost about 20 pounds due to foreign sanctions. It was a tough time. The government had to figure out how to produce everything their people needed from right there on the island. Which is why all the cars are American cars from the 1950s. They learned how to make use of what they had. It doesn't sound like a happy or comfortable time for them. Contrarily, the younger people seem to be much happier with their situation. As long as they do something to contribute to their community, the Cuban system meets all of their basic needs. Food, lodging, transportation, health care... I mean, they're communist, so that's the good part of communism. One of the negatives is that they don't get any information from the outside world. Which is why they LOVE tourists. They just want to ask us questions to try to get an idea of what else is going on in the world besides the Guarda with machine guns. Because of the censorship in their media outlets, they have this belief that all Americans are rich, have enormous houses, and lots of cars. And then us white gringos show up on sailboats, with money—maybe not a lot, but still more than they have—and drink and party all day! So their ideas don't seem so wrong, really.

But somehow, they're still very HAPPY. I mean, ridiculously happy. The kind of happy that you would never find in an American tourist town. At least not from my experience! It has been a very surprising welcome to experience such authentic generosity.

Jan 24, 01
Cayo Rosario, Cuba

Curried lentil soup tonight. It was my turn to cook, and I got the highest compliment from Elizabeth:

"Would have been wonderful even if we weren't on the boat!"

Considering that one of the first rules-of-thumb we came up with once we got to Cuba and realized how sparse the rationings were, was that you could say anything you wanted about anyone's cooking—such as "This is the worst shit I've ever tasted" – as long as it was followed by, "Good, though!"

In this manner, we were free to be both realistic about our negativity and supportive in our positivity at the same time!

***

Sitting in an unprotected anchorage tonight, and the winds are almost 20 knots. Plenty of night checks will be had tonight, and not much restful sleep.

We crossed paths with a couple of other boats today and had the binoculars out, searching to find some socializing opportunities for at least a night. To no avail. We're still all alone in our windy, spacious anchorage. Cayo Largo soon...

The situation on board is on the upswing. Both Elizabeth and I have sufficiently flipped out on Richard enough that he is now somewhat chilling out. This morning he actually stayed in bed while Liz and I got everything ready to go. Got the dinghy on deck and lashed down, the cabin squared away, the charts out and courses plotted, the engine started, anchor up and sails full... Then he joined us at the helm, although I know it was killing him to trust us without his authoritative opinions being bounced around. And might I add, we did a tremendous job! Way to go, us!

Jan 27, 2001
Cayo Largo, Cuba

Shitty day on the water today. 20 to 25 knots dead on and seas at about 6 feet. But neither Liz nor I got sick, and I actually took a reef out by myself, even if it did take me 20 fucking minutes. And we decided to tie up to a slip at the dock tonight. Luxury! I wish a picture could capture what this place feels like. There is music, Cuban music, in the background. The temp is around 80 degrees. The sun is about to set, and there are friendly people everywhere. Tonight, there is a fiesta in the middle square, about 50 feet from where the boat sits at dock. Today, after we docked, we walked by this yacht, and the guy on board was scrubbing and washing the entire thing down. All I could think was how grateful I am that I didn't take that fucking yacht job out of Ft. Lauderdale with that horny captain. That could easily have been me doing the scrubbing. No, thank you!

Tonight, I will partake in mucho fiesta and tomorrow sleep late. No pulling anchor at sunrise. No making tea, no helm shifts... I'm grateful for the break. Life could be much worse!

***

A very high compliment from Elizabeth the other day... "You could crack a walnut with that ass!" Ah... friends... I'm the one who pulls anchor from every anchorage. Sometimes, when you have the wind and the currents in your favor, it's not a lot of work. It can actually be pretty easy on the muscles. But, other times, it's like pulling up a 60 lb. deadweight from upwards of 30 feet. It was one such morning that Elizabeth was standing behind me, and I, clad in my thong bathing suit (which is actually more than usual on this boat) was busy at my task of pulling anchor. At which point, said comment was voiced. Thanks, Elizabeth. I may be a tad overweight for my own comfort, but I will admit that I am one strong chica!

Jan 29, 01
Cayo Rosario

Following seas today, winds at about 15-20 knots and seas were pretty big and rolly. Amazingly, neither Elizabeth nor I got even the slightest bit queasy. We both took a ginger pill before we left. It seemed to have worked. No sickness for either of us. And now we sit at a bumpy anchorage with fishermen right next to us. And I mean RIGHT next to us. Not really sure what they're doing, but they came out of nowhere, with no one else in sight, and tied up to the boat. More than slightly unsettling, seeing as how they pulled right up beside us, tied up, and then went about their own business in their cabin. No jovial greeting. Not even a miniscule hello. But they don't seem to be any threat. They're in the cabin making food. We think they're cooking us a meal. I'm glad I'm not alone right now. I guess we'll see what happens...

Well, we reached a unanimous decision to extend our visas yesterday. So we'll be cruising the south coast for approximately 7 more days before returning to Florida. The visa thing is funny here. Since Elizabeth and I have US passports, and according to the US, it is illegal for us to be here, the Cubans know how to make this work. Actually, the US law says that it's illegal for us to "spend money" on Cuban soil. And they know Cuba charges for an entry visa. Hence, it's illegal for us to get into their country. But the Cubans, being very opportunistic, have figured out a way to make it work for everyone involved, besides the US government, that is. Upon arrival at a port, they stamp a piece of paper and staple it into our passport. Then, upon leaving those waters, they just take the paper out. They get their entry fee. We get to be there. And there's no trace for the US government upon return to the States. Very clever, those Cubans!

Oh, and yes, the fishermen cooked us a fantastic meal of lobster and rice in trade for some rum. We all had a great time trying to understand each other over the yummy crustacean and realized they were looking for rum. Which, of course, we always have on board because you never know when a lobster boat will cruise up out of nowhere, tie off to the boat, and cook you a lobster meal. All for want of rum. It's always good to be prepared.

Cayo Largo was our last port. Two nights and lots of money gone by! The first night we were lucky enough to be there in time for a huge party happening in the town square. There must have been 200 people or more enjoying the festivities. After the fanfare in the main square, it was off to the discotheque. After that experience, I am thoroughly convinced that every single Cuban citizen, whether they male or female, young or old, has rhythm in their blood. They are ALL excellent dancers! Such a welcome difference from the nightlife in the States, where young white men have no idea what to do on a dance floor. There is a good basis for the saying "white man overbite."

The rum and the dancing were a much welcome break from the monotony of the usual isolated anchorage. All three of us had a fantastically fun night! Got to bed at 4 am, alone, much to the chagrin of the little Cuban man who followed me around all night. And woke up with a nasty hangover. Ah, rum, why is this such a one-sided relationship? Such is the price of fun while on a tropical island. Time to rescue the bread from the oven now.

Jan 30, 01
Cayo Rosario

This entire trip has been the ultimate test of patience and happiness. Be careful what you ask for... The energies between the three of us are so strong. Not necessarily good either. It's hard to stay in my power when I'm so tempted to be slung through all of their mind games: with each other and with me. I'm learning just to hide in my cabin when things get weird, which happens more frequently now. I'm so in need of human contact, but am unwilling to settle for something purely sexual. It hasn't even been that long, but having to watch these two interact with each other in front of me, 24/7, for six weeks straight, makes me long for what I obviously am not getting. I feel like I'm open to it, ready for it, welcoming it... It will come...

8:20 pm and I'm lying in bed again. Welcome to life on a boat.

Feb 2, 01
Cayo Mattais

Writing by the light of the moon tonight. Just finished a dinner of fresh red snapper caught on our way into the anchorage. The catch was classic. We were about 20 feet away from a passing sailboat. Richard was at the helm and Elizabeth sitting in the cockpit with him, waving to the six people on their deck, when I hooked something off the back deck. The scene didn't take too long, but shortly after the bite, it was pretty epic to be pulling the line up to reveal a ten-pound snapper, strolling the deck of the boat in a sarong, while being cheered on and waved at from the passing boat. No rod, only a line on a spool. What a scene for my ego to feed off of. That fish couldn't have made us look any better!

And now, as so many times before, we sit here stuffed like happy little pigs at the trough. The last two days have been excellent. Two days ago, we sailed out of our anchorage at Cayo Rosario with no motor and proceeded to sail our way through shallow, crystal clear waters dotted with various reefs along the way. Elizabeth and I took turns climbing the mast and relaxing on the spreaders, looking for coral heads to avoid. We took a midday stop to anchor and snorkel, and Richard caught a lobster and speared some fish for our midday snack. Then, anchored by Cayo Avolos, they took the dinghy ashore while I swam, and wandered the rocky beaches in search of iguanas and monkeys. We did get to see a few iguanas, but the monkeys, we were told, were up in the forest canopy and didn't seem to want to come visit with us.

Both Elizabeth and I were trying to translate what the Cuban guy was telling us. It was during that process that I realized how utterly terrible my Spanish really is. Mine came out something like, "The water crocodiles scare away the monkeys at this time of day." Hers was way closer to the truth, which is that the monkeys went inland to the treetops in the daytime and only came out to the coast at night. Where the hell did I come up with crocodiles? My Spanish still sucks.

***

My cabin in Alaska was forgotten history as I floated naked in these opaque waters off the Cuban coast. On this morning, I had elected to swim ashore and leave the necessities for my daily island excursion to Richard and Elizabeth to take in the dinghy for me. They were already wandering around the deserted island and out of sight. The grassy reeds of the ocean floor kept getting closer and closer to my torso as the depths became quite shallow. So shallow that at one point I could touch the bottom with my fingertips while swimming but didn't want to walk due to the abundant sea grass. Just at about this point, I looked directly below me, and through my goggles realized I was looking directly into the eyes of a stingray, laying nicely covered in sand on the ocean floor. He was bedded down in the sand just enough so I could see his eyes clearly, slightly sticking up from the sandy bottom, but the rest of his body was less than a faint outline on the sea floor, waiting for his next meal to swim by. I was hoping it wasn't me! Considering that we mutually startled each other in our surprise introduction, I had no choice but to trust that this beautiful creature was indeed not going to kill me with its deadly tail. Increased heart rate is not easily dealt with when breathing through a plastic snorkel. And I unquestionably had a racing heart! Along with my adrenaline rush was a huge curiosity, a feeling of magic, and an immense sense of gratitude. It was only him (maybe her; I had no idea) and I, having a moment together, in this dazzling place he called home. The tropical sun shone down through the crystal-clear water, giving the ray an otherworldly glow. I had only one option, and that was to just keep swimming. Making sure that my body remained as flat on the surface of the water as possible. It was one of those moments in life that fill the soul with overwhelming awe. Even though I was scared shitless (not literally, thank God) the communication between the sea creature and I was unmistakable. Luckily, he decided I wasn't a threat, and we remained in eye contact as I carefully swam over him to my beach destination. When I got to shore, I stood on the sand, looking his way, and did a silent blessing for our magical meeting. There wasn't another soul for miles (human, anyway), and it honored me to make this winged sea creature's acquaintance. This was between us. I never mentioned it to either Richard or Elizabeth.

***

Our plans for leaving the following morning were diverted after meeting our new friends on the "Pirrata" - Nils and David. The next morning, we all piled on board Coquette and sailed out to the old shipwreck, about a mile out from where we were both anchored, and snorkeled for the day. Once again, crystal clear water and loads of colorful reef fish enchanted us, and better yet, wonderful company and conversation had with other cruisers. The underwater cannons of the shipwreck we snorkeled around were quite mind-blowing. It really got me to thinking about the specifics of the scene. Obviously, the ship sank while undertaking some kind of fight. What were they fighting about? Who was fighting? Where were the fighters from? Were they local or from a faraway port? Had they been at sea for a while or were their families near to where the ship went down? The depth of the water was only about twelve to fifteen feet, the water was warm, and land was within a mile. I'm sure that whoever lived through the battle could have swum to shore. But then what? So many questions and so few answers. Their story will remain a mystery within the wreck of the ship only twelve feet from the water's surface, in an area that sees very few visitors, off an almost deserted coast of an island in the middle of the Caribbean. Questions that have answers only to those no longer living...

All five of us joined forces for dinner and had a feast of grouper and conch over pasta and proceeded onto a drawn-out game of cards until 11 pm. They made our day by bringing over their radio, and we listened to the wonderful sounds of CDs all night. Danced to Bob Marley on deck for an hour before dragging my bedding up to fall asleep under the moon and stars. We awoke this morning to say our goodbyes over coffee, and we were off once again.

It was slow going today, with the wind dead behind us, but we got to partake in putting up the spinnaker. Besides the weird energy between the three of us, the sailing was hot and relaxing. I have a feeling there was some jealous energy happening between Elizabeth and Richard, but, as usual, I just tuned it out in order to make my life onboard more bearable. Tonight blessed us with fresh snapper, which we gave half of to the Swiss family anchored next to us. And now I sit under the moon enjoying the crystal water and gentle breeze. It's hard to conceive of what Alaska weather is like at this moment!

Feb 3, 2001
Somewhere on a Boat

I don't find it fair that it's called gaining weight. I mean, in one sense, yes, my body is "gaining" excess fat. But in another sense, I really don't feel that I've gained anything by some additional fat on my midsection. And losing it is another term that doesn't really fit. I don't feel a sense of loss when that excess weight is gone. More like, LATER! Don't let the door hit you in the ass on the way out! And this whole yo-yo thing... Gaining and losing... Feeling like crap about myself and then feeling like a Goddess again... It's all a bit much. Not that I mind being on the Goddess side of that swing, which I'm not right now. Ugh... But being stuck on the boat is challenging. Not the best situation for getting physical activity! And, somehow, it always seems that there's plenty of alcohol around. Hmm... Rum is not necessarily a diet drink!

This past 5 weeks has been a beguiling experience, with its pros and cons, but I must admit that I am thankful that the end is drawing near. Another long, drawn out day of mind games on board. Spent most of the evening trying not to take on the negative energy of these two confused souls and couldn't help but to get lost in thoughts of Alaska again. I really miss Josh and wonder often about what he's doing up there. He showed me how great it feels to not accept someone else's energy. Now I realize few people are capable of that, including me at the present moment! This must be in the top ten for most trying times for me. I don't think I have ever felt so invisible and unvalidated in my life. Patience and happiness... Really good goals to strive for...

Putting myself in their shoes, this has to be hard for them, too. Going on a sailing trip to an illegal foreign country with someone you've only known for a few days, most of that time in a drunken haze, is a bit of a risky scenario. Like any new relationship, the physical attraction is obviously powerful. They do have that going for them! It's a good thing my berth is in the stern and not up in the main cabin with them. There's only so much I can take! But the day-to-day stuff is something that doesn't come fast or easy. And they jumped right into it. And currently, it's not so smooth.

Elizabeth has nicknamed me "The Muse" on this voyage. For me, it feels quite the opposite. I feel invisible to them, with no needs, no emotions, no wants or desires. Just here, taking up space and sometimes getting in their way of unhindered sex. It's a very interesting phenomenon, to be so close to two other people for such a long time without ever really feeling noticed.

The juxtaposition of personal space and physical touch, or in this case a lack thereof, is perplexing and confusing to my psyche. My physical needs have been completely anesthetized at this point, yet with three of us living on a 44-foot boat, personal space is at a minimum, to say the least!

A fascinating situation, indeed...

Feb 4, 01
Punta Frances

So many thoughts floating through my head... We are coming to the end of our Cuban travels. The imminent future holds a four or five day sail back to Ft. Lauderdale to check back into the good old US of A. We have gotten so spoiled with hot, beautiful, sunny weather that the prospect of going back to Florida looks cold and bleak. I'm thinking of catching the next plane, either to Colorado or maybe Mexico, if Jim is on the boat there. Ah, Jim... The one who started this entire boating excursion off. Wow, how crazy it is to look back on situations and how things find a way to pull together. Was it really just a few months ago that I jumped into Jim's camper? From Alaska to Mexico was the plan. But only got as far as Phoenix and then got sidetracked and ended up on the East coast, and now I'm sitting on a South African boat in Cuban waters. Because, of course, I would... What else would I be doing? Isn't this how all people live?! Geez... One thing is for certain, nobody can ever call me boring.

Later

I'm on the second shift of anchor watch this evening, from midnight to 3 am. There's a slight breeze, and the boat is slightly swinging off the hook, but nothing really to worry about. As long as I don't fall asleep on my shift and then Coquette decides to pull a bit too hard and drag us into shore, or something similarly unwanted, I'll be good tonight. Still having thoughts of the Cuban excursion coming to an end. Ironically, it's been fascinating, challenging, and exhilarating all at once. Most definitely an experience that I will carry for a lifetime! And hopefully the memories of these hot summer days playing in the salty seawaters of the Cuban coast will get me through a few more harsh Alaskan winters. If that's even where I end up again.

In the meantime, tomorrow is a relaxing day of snorkeling, probably our last, and wandering around the cliffs of this beautiful coast. Sometime in the evening, we set sail for our departure town, Maria la Gorda, which is about a seventeen-hour sail from here. It looks like favorable weather for our sail there, and then we're hoping for another good weather window to tackle the crossing. More paperwork from both sides, exiting Cuba and entering back into the states. Icky bureaucratic crap...

But for tonight, I am reveling in the starlight and soothing sound of the slight breeze and the waves softly lapping against the hull.

Feb 5, 01
Maria La Gorda

Just returned to the boat from a night out drinking Cuban rum at the hotel bar we are anchored closest to. Richard and Elizabeth are constantly trying to get me laid. But they don't get it, I don't want to! Yes, I am starving for some physical touch. But I would like it to come in the form of connection and possibly some intimacy with another person. Another night trying to brush off unwanted advances from another lost, drunk, horny soul. This one was from Mauritius, I think. He was actually pretty rocked, but lately all I can think about is Josh. Wanting the security and comfort of his presence, both of us back in the cabin again...

Oh well, we leave this country tomorrow and end our five-week voyage. Another week on the boat, and then it's off to another adventure. I hope the weather is better than it was coming over here—25 knots and 6-foot seas beam-on; it was horrendous! I ended my three hours at the helm, tired and wet, and sick of being sick. The beneficial aspect was the constant 7 ½ knots. We got here in about twelve hours instead of the sixteen it was supposed to take, but definitely rough going. If we get four days of that on the way back, it's going to be hell! For now, I have my fair share of Cuban rum in me, have smoked way too many cigarettes, and need to sleep. Alone.

Feb 10, 2001
Key West, Florida

I slowly open my eyes and think to myself, "Am I dead? Is this death?"

My body is no longer being tossed to and fro in my berth. There is no pounding of waves against the side of the boat. No constant rocking from the anger of the seas. For the moment, at least, I do not have to run for the rails in order to violently empty my stomach, or what remains of my stomach to empty.

All of these things would make it seem that I have succumbed to death. Yet, I find a slight solace in the fact that I am still wet and uncomfortable. This simple fact alone lets me know that the grips of darkness have not overtaken me. Not yet, anyway. And I am grateful for the wetness and discomfort that confirms my alive-ness. I have no clue how long I have been laying here in my berth. What I do know is that it is light outside, and the onslaught of waves against the hull has seemingly stopped. The energy of the boat actually seems pleasant, which, admittedly, I didn't really think I would ever feel again! Wow, they were a horrendously rough few days! I have a feeling that I didn't make it to my last helm shift. But they never came to wake me. So, I really don't know how long I've been asleep. But I do remember how absolutely seasick I was before disappearing into my berth. Puking for three days straight, on a boat that is constantly getting hit by waves and rocking back and forth, is not a pleasant experience. Really, I wasn't sure about that whole death thing.

When I finally muster the energy to stick my head above board, both Richard and Elizabeth were uncertain of whether I still remained in the realm of the living either. They actually seemed much more relieved than I to find that I was, in fact, still alive. Not only was I still alive, but I had stopped hurling my guts up as well. Oh, the joy!

I look around to find that the entire contents of the living quarters have been spread out on deck to dry. Everything, every single thing, that could have gotten wet, is drenched and has been for days. Cushions, sheets, clothes, rugs, towels, etc... Miscellaneous items are hanging on every line and rail possible, soaking up whatever sun is available to evaporate some of the wretched seawater from things. The sun is shining; the winds are calm, and these three cruisers are happy and smiling currently. This is a prime example of "You can't know light without experiencing dark."

Later

After waking back to the land of the living, all three of us are happily soaking up the calm seas and sunshine on deck when we notice a bunch of boats traveling quickly in the opposite direction. With a quick glance ahead, we simultaneously notice a huge, threatening thundercloud. There is a squall coming directly for us. Now, this is definitely bad news for most people on the water, but not for us. With a quick and knowing glance shared, we all jump into action! Moving fast, we stretch out a tarp to use as a rain catch, with a bucket at the end of the declining material. The soap and shampoo are quickly retrieved from the head shower and placed on deck, and we head straight for the middle of the squall, deliriously determined to get clean. Fresh water, in whatever form it is given, is a Godsend, and there is no way we are going to miss that chance! The other boaters all think we're crazy and keep screaming at us to turn around, to go the other way... But all we see is a welcomed and abundant gift of heavenly, saltless, water.

As the squall hits us, head-on, we are all naked and ready. Shampoo already soaping up our heads, the tarp already filling our bucket, and all of our salt drenched wares are being blessedly anointed with clean, fresh rainwater. I do believe that I have never been so appreciative of pouring rain in my life!

Feb 12, 01
Key West

We checked in with customs and INS yesterday morning. Despite all the threats and warnings we got before leaving the country, no one really seemed to care about us traveling to Cuba. No questions, and a quick stamp in the passport. They didn't even come to the boat. We had to go to them at their airport office. Absolutely no one would have known or cared if we checked in or not. It was actually kind of ironic; we hitched a ride to the airport with a Cuban couple who picked us up in their beat-up truck. When we all piled into the truck and saw the Cuban flag hanging from the rear-view mirror, we were excitedly trying to explain to them that we had just gotten back from a visit to their country. Initially, they denied being from Cuba (seeing as how they feared the INS, who we might actually be), but then Richard offered them a cigar (literally, straight off the boat), and they were suddenly all smiles! Happy and laughing along with us, and telling us proud stories of their country for the short ride to the airport office... It was a small reminder of the happiness that all Cubans seem to exude.

After checking back in to the States, we are now passing our time in Key West, partying and drinking way too much again. Those blue drinks are just so good! Unfortunately for me, the mind games and unsettling energy coming from these two lost souls is getting to be too much. We have one more leg of the trip, from here to St. Augustine, and I'm beginning to believe that I may have to bail on them before that. I was able to check my email yesterday for the first time in a while, and got word from Jim, who is back in Mexico working on his boat at dry dock. His original cruising offer still stands, and it's beyond tempting to check out and leave these two to their own sordid relationship antics. But I just got my friend Hank to send all my mail from Alaska to Elizabeth's place in St. Augustine, and I gave Richard my word that I would finish the trip with him. This whole thing is dragging on too long for my liking, though, and I don't know what to do. We're stuck in Key West until the winds change, which could be another three days or so, and then it's going to take another three or four days to get up the coast. I really don't think I can handle it anymore, being the third wheel and the muse.

I'm going to have to get a lift into town tomorrow and see if Jim has answered my email yet. Yet again, I'm faced with whatever the next creation may be?

2:45 am Feb 13
Key West

Woke up half an hour ago and am still laying here with my eyes wide open. Elizabeth and I sat up for an hour after Richard went to bed, reminiscing of our disgusting, but hysterical, stories of our experiences of the last crossing. We were laughing so hard we were crying! Who would have known that puking or taking a shit could be so damned funny?!

Being awoken at midnight for a three-hour helm shift you know is going to be a living hell. Lurching for the autopilot button while trying to make it to the leeward deck in time to find that after puking for 36 hours, the only thing left to come up is the lining of your stomach— which, by the way, looks like coffee grounds. Then the low battery alarm sounds and you have to, somehow, stop yourself from the upheaval of stomach lining to lurch back to the auto-helm button and throw yourself down the companionway to turn on the ignition switch to the engine in order to juice up the battery again. All the while getting slammed around in eight-foot seas and trying not to fall overboard. At which point you actually enjoy getting drenched by beam-on waves since they eliminate the need for tissues! Meanwhile, your body is not so subtly giving you reminders that you haven't used the head in two days. But this brings on the nagging realization that if you dare to go down below deck (which is where the head happens to be) you will have to stop vomiting long enough to get that accomplished. Knowing that going down below for any amount of time in these seas will send you back up on deck to start the whole running-for-the-rails episode all over again. But you succumb to mother nature because she's been calling for two days and won't be ignored for much longer. Lurch for that godsent autopilot button again, throw your body in the general direction of the head and pray that the stomach will wait its turn. As you're pulling up your wet jeans, one of those eight-foot waves slams into the side of the boat and sends you flying into the door of the head, which, of course, proceeds to let go of its hinges, and sends you flying across the boat and into the middle cabin. The captain comes screaming in to find out if you're still alive just in time to see the vision of you laying against the head door, jeans around your ankles, trying to get up in time to make it back into the cockpit before you start to puke again.

Only another two hours left of your helm shift before you get to go back to your sopping wet bunk and strap yourself in for another 6 hours of being thrown around in your sleep.

And I voluntarily signed up for this! I think my mother was right all along; I have a few screws loose.

Valentine's Day 2001

Waiting, yet again, for the winds to change
Eating and drinking too much
Moving less and less
Being bored out of my mind
Staring at other boats in the anchorage and wondering
what their stories are
Wondering when this trip will finally come to an end
I think my time is up
I want off

Later

I have got to get to town so I can spend some time on the internet. Looking up all kinds of possibilities for my next step. Maybe conservationism, maybe organic farming, maybe sea turtles or dolphins or whale volunteer programs, maybe ecotourism. Somehow, I would love to get involved in giving back instead of just taking all the time. Not that the past few months haven't been an incredible experience, but I would like to work for the greater good somehow. In the big picture, I would like to be making a difference in some way. Maybe I should just be thinking about getting back to Alaska. Get situated and stable for a while again... But my mind isn't quite in Alaska mode yet. It's so much more exciting to conjure up more adventures!

It's amazing how one choice, big or small, can change the path of your entire existence. Just one choice. What if Richard and I didn't get along when we first met? I never would have been on this boat, and most likely would never have gone to Cuba. What if I had taken that job on the yacht instead? Wow! My life would look very different right now.

Just one choice, and down the rabbit hole I go...

Feb 15, 2001
The Exit

I did it. Made the tough choice. Here I sit, on a bench at the marina at 7 am. I woke up on Coquette, about an hour ago, and still had that horrible feeling in the pit of my stomach. It could have been my gut telling me to go. It could have been the Universe giving me a heads up I had to go. Maybe it was intuition that knew there was something bad coming. Or maybe it was just that I couldn't stand another day on that boat. For whatever reason, I left. I tried to explain to Richard why I had to get off the boat. That I had been ignoring my feelings for the past two months and this one was simply too strong to be pushed down. So, I packed my things, called the water taxi on the radio, said my goodbyes, and left. And now I sit on a bench at the marina, with my entire life at my feet in the contents of two backpacks. It's 7 am, I don't have a clue what to do or where to go. I could just go to the airport or Greyhound station, but I'm not sure what my destination would be. Maybe just go to a hostel nearby. But I have the entire day, and that would be a waste of money if I decide not to stay.

What now? Jersey to visit family/Colorado/Mexico with Jim/back to Alaska/or somewhere totally different? No, I'm done for this time around. I've been gone from Alaska for four months and am ready for a bit of stability again. I'm going to check on Jersey flights today and maybe see the family for a few and then head back to my life.

***

It's surreal to me that I left them! I'm struggling with guilt. Richard desperately wanted to get back to South Africa for his sister's wedding, and when I left this morning, he wasn't even sure if they were going to sail or not. It's going to be hard for Elizabeth to handle her half of the work, and he knows it. But she stood with me all the way. She's going to forward my mail and send me copies of all the pictures. It all ended congenially with hugs and promises to keep in touch... I just can't help feeling completely overwhelmed with guilt over leaving them somewhat high and dry. Or maybe I'm giving myself too much credit and they'll be fantastically better without me on board. Who knows? But after two months of not paying attention to my needs at all, this horrible feeling would not get pushed aside. And God knows, I tried! Maybe this is just another one of my personal lessons to be true to myself, first and foremost.

Later

I'm sure I look totally ridiculous, walking around all wobbly and such, like a drunken slob. I believe the correct terminology for this malady is "disembarkment syndrome." That's when you've been living on a boat for a long period of time and have gotten so used to swaying and bobbing with the rolling water that when you finally reach land, you still walk with the sways and bobs of being on water. I wonder how long before this wears off and I can walk on solid ground without swaggering back and forth like a drunkard. It really is quite ridiculous!

I remember Richard telling the story of their kitten, Coquette (aptly named after the boat). Richard, his brother, and his sister-in-law were getting the boat ready for their big crossing, South Africa to Norfolk, VA, when they decided to get a kitten for some company on the voyage. It took them just over three months to complete the sail. And when Coquette finally stepped on land after the voyage, the now grown cat would run in 44 ft lengths, then turn around and run back 44 ft, and so on and so on. Since she had led her entire life on a 44 ft boat, that's the only thing she knew. 44 feet. Poor cat.

After this experience, I can completely understand how that cat felt! I wonder if I'll miss the sounds of the water slapping the hull when I close my eyes now that I'm no longer ocean bound.

Feb 25, 2001
Cherry Hill NJ

Back at Mom's house now, laying in my old bed, in my old room, among my old things. Weird. How does it come to be that my personal items from high school still remain entrapped in this room? Like a mausoleum. I'm 30 years old. Shouldn't they have disappeared by now, all these left behind, forgotten remnants of my past years? Just weird.

I spent the last week and a half at various family members' homes, and I'm now looking forward to seeing Mike and Jen in Phoenix for a quick visit, and then it's down to Mexico to help Jim get the boat seaworthy. It was good to see the family, especially the nieces and nephews, but it's even better to be on my way again. Coming back "home" always sends me headlong into an emotional uproar, but this time seems to be somewhat manageable, and I'm grateful for the inner peace around it all. At least I didn't have to get any Valium from Alison this time around! Thank God for high school friends with soothing drugs.

Feb 27, 2001
Chicago Airport

Mom dropped me off at the Philly airport this morning. After drinking too much wine all night at Alison and

Steve's house, my head was whirling, and I thought I might puke. Then I had to put up with Mom and her glorified stories all morning. As the years wear on, her stories get longer and more imaginative and have a tendency to slowly drive the listener to an unbearable sort of insanity. It's such a shame, because she's old, and old people have so much history. So many stories and information. It could be so interesting to learn of her past. But that's not what she talks about. It's like she's talking at you, instead of with you. And I certainly never feel like she hears a word I say. But then my sisters tell me later that she called them and told them all about me. And I thought she heard nothing from me. Ah, family communication... Rarely evolved...

Seeing Alison and Steve again was fun. She's four and a half months pregnant with #2, and they are already planning their third! It's amazing to me, such a different life... But we still manage to stay pretty close, having respect for our differences, and I appreciate that immensely!

And now back to Phoenix, and possibly to see Jim for a week in Mexico. What I'm most excited about is stopping in Colorado for a while to visit with Deb. Then it's back up to Alaska. I've started looking online for summer jobs up there and am psyched to get to see Boomer again and take him on beach walks! I wonder how Josh is doing and what he'll be up to when I get back.

3/1/01
Phoenix

Presently, I'm sitting at a bus station in Phoenix, Arizona, waiting for a bus to take me across the border to Guaymas, Mexico. I am completely prepared to be holding chickens or dealing with bleating goats if need be, but fortunately for me, it looks like these buses are pretty cush. Actually, they look a lot better than your average American Greyhound bus. I don't foresee any chickens or goats in my near future. Not gonna be an African-bus-travel kind of day...

Just spent a few days in Phoenix with Jen and Mike and kids. It's been a long time since our old party days back in good old Colorado! Ah... reminiscing was fun, though! Good to see them. Once again, I'm so grateful to have people in my life who are following a completely different path but seem to have acceptance and respect enough for me to still be a part of their world every once in a while.

The plan is, another month, and then it's back to the stability of Alaska. Well, my version of "stable," anyway! A quick visit in Phoenix, a week in Mexico, then back to Colorado to visit with Deb and friends, final destination–Alaska.

The week with Jim will be a welcome respite from putting my own needs aside. Although I am supposedly going down to help him restore his wooden sailboat, I somehow foresee little work getting done. If anything, at least I know there is some mutual attraction there. Whatever happens, I'm open... Physical contact is well overdue in my world! After months of no physical contact, I'm actually slightly nervous about getting attention from a man. Here's to my reality being back rubs and physical tenderness. Maybe some heavy breathing and sweaty stuff too, but I don't want to jinx myself!

3/3/01
Somewhere near Guaymas, Mexico

I'm here! In Mexico! With Jim! And it's wonderful!

Today we went walking on the beach, just after sunrise. The sun was bright and beautiful over the ocean, and not yet unbearably hot. Walking in the sand was a temperate trick on the toes. The top was warm due to the just risen sunshine, but just underneath the surface, it was still cold from the chill of the night. My toes were very confused! But it felt super cool, like an odd temperature sensation for my feet. We probably walked for a few miles before we made our way back to the camper van parked not far from the waterline. It wasn't until we were parked at the sailboat in drydock that we realized something was amiss. Jim noticed his wallet wasn't where he left it, and then when he found it, realized that it was empty of cash. That wasn't how it was left. Then I went to check on my little purse that I had left under the couch cushions in the back of the van. Mine was empty, too. We were complete idiots, and in our blissed-out state, we completely forgot to lock the doors. Stupid gringos... They got a total of $250 from us, most of it coming from my purse, unfortunately for me. Utterly fortunate for both of us was that just the cash was missing. We both still had our passports, credit cards, IDs; they even left the condoms untouched–thank god. It was a very respectful theft. Nothing was out of place, no mess. We were pretty lucky. As far as thieves go, they were easy on us!

Other than the inconvenience of a robbery, it's great to be here. The weather is fantastic, and the sex is more than commendable. We're cooking dinner, drinking beer, and waiting to watch the sunset over the beach. The original plan was to leave here next week, but since things are going so well (besides the misfortune of being ripped off), we both like the idea of staying longer. There's no pressure or timeframe to get back to Alaska, and his job as a tugboat captain doesn't have him scheduled for at least a few weeks. Free as birds! Neither of us thought we would enjoy each other's company as much as we are, so we'll draw it out a little longer. We're even playing around with some schemes for the future that would help our financial situations. He's got property on a remote Alaskan island out in the Sound somewhere, and with a bit of hard work, there are some great financial opportunities that we could feasibly make happen. One day at a time... Admittedly, it feels so fulfilling to ponder some crazy, yet utterly possible, schemes with another kind of off the wall personality!

3/5/01
San Carlos, Mexico

Simplicity. Serenity.
Calm Seas. Blue Water.
Pelicans. Fishermen.
Immense passion and fear of the unknown, no, not fear exactly, but apprehension.

So many times, I am lost in the moment and forget about creating the next experience. Like floating about in outer space, but still enjoying the view. The whole point being, I get myself into these crazy, far out, cool situations where everything is different and new, but if I look into the future, I might get scared. So I choose to live in the moment. But then I forget that in order to create the next phase, I have to step out of the present. Present, like a gift. Or pre-sent, as in preordained. A bunch of different perspectives...

Fear is ever existent, and one must strive to leaps and bounds to overcome it. Then again, fear is a potent motivator in some circumstances.

Lust, passion, soul searching, sex, friendship, longing, solitude, union, emotion–CONFUSION.

Later

On a very different topic, I just need to vent about how people react to my stories of Cuba. Specifically, American people. It's absolutely fucking amazing to me how many people have told me I'm wrong. That Cuba is horrible. That the people are all dying and being tortured on a daily basis.

I JUST CAME from there. I spent weeks and week there. I mean, REALLY?! It's amazing how many people have completely discredited my EXPERIENCES – not my opinions, not my stories, but my actual experiences, due to their misinformed and skewed beliefs. Beliefs are not facts. Americans are so fucking ignorant about anything but their own bubble. It's really quite infuriating! Okay, okay... I'll get over it...

Rant over. For now.

3/7/01
San Carlos, Mexico

Tonight is our last night here in this quaint little Mexican town on the coast. I've only been here for a week, but this has been Jim's home for over two months. We made a joint decision today that we would both love to be snowboarding for the next few weeks and get the best of both worlds. Seize this opportunity, now that we have the chance. So, it's time to move Northward. First stop, Phoenix. Most probably, visit with Jen, Mike, and the kids for a night on our way through, and then on to my beloved Rocky Mountains. It's very convenient having my sister as a base there! Here we come, Deb and Art!

This week has been full of fun, yet still sort of uncomfortable on a certain level. Lots of sex and an overload of attention, which is a refreshing and a welcome difference, but something I am NOT accustomed to! After four months of getting almost no attention on the boat with Richard and Elizabeth, I am now thrown into an overabundance. As has been true for most of my life, there is rarely a stable middle ground. It's usually all or nothing. As my friend, Karen, in Colorado would say, "GRAY, girl!! Where's the GRAY!! It's not always black and white!!" Bless you, dear Karen... There might be hope for me yet...

3/11/01
Utah somewhere

Red rocks and scrub oaks surround our little, actually it's not so little, camper van, in the middle of this wild and magnificent setting. Yesterday morning, I got breakfast in bed, topped off with a single red rose to make me feel better. It's colder here than further south, and my body has taken to revolting. Basically, I have a nasty cold. Jim did a magnificent job at brightening up my gloominess!

And now he's yapping on about this Alaska Island Wilderness Camp idea, and all I want to do is write.

Oh, poor me... I guess I'll put some wind in his sails, so to speak.

Later

Past, Present, and Future—Ant, Otter, and Hummingbird

I haven't pulled my animal medicine cards in quite a while, and it's been well overdue. It feels soul fulfilling to get myself back into a bit of a spiritual space again. This morning we saw a hummingbird sitting in the tree outside the camper window, and all day I've been having one of those extremely grateful days. Appreciation and gratitude are oozing from my soul. I take a petal from my rose and rub it on my face for hours, just noticing how soft it feels against my skin. Every horizon I gaze at has the possibility to be wondrous when reached. I feel so thankful to be alive today. It's a good day to be me! Blessed Be...

3/12/01
Canyonlands in Utah

It's happening again. He's falling in love, and I want out. The sex was great for the first bit, and then... well... We both love to travel. He has his own boat, loves to sail, and also has property twenty miles out from Seward on the ocean and wants to do an ecotourism thing out there. He wants my help and is open to doing it together. This all sounds absolutely wonderful and it would be, except for the fact that he's driving me nutty! We both have this control thing going on, and it's causing a lot of conflict. But then, I think maybe it's me. This happens often. This same scenario. And the one constant is ME. No matter what guy it is, there always seems to be something not quite right. Like a square peg trying to fit in a round hole. I have "the grass is always greener on the other side" syndrome. I keep thinking about Josh and how good it was at one time. Communication was not his strong point, along with intimacy. Not sex, but intimacy. And there I go again, always finding something wrong.

Jim is really trying. That much is apparent. He's always cooking and making me coffee and breakfast in bed. And the eye contact–oh, the eye contact! –is new and refreshing! That's always what I wanted from Josh that he just couldn't give me. Now I've got it with someone else, and I don't want the someone else. What the hell is up with that??? What am I looking for??? What do I need??? Fucking hell...

Later

The burnt oranges and reds of the canyon lands are mesmerizing and beautiful. Lizards scurry from underfoot, and the sun blazes her fiery rays upon us mere humans down here, partaking of the desert landscape. This place is magical, yet extreme and challenging. The days are hot and the nights are cold. Dessert flora and fauna are tough, able to withstand extreme temperature changes in such a short period of time and live without water for long periods. It's a beautiful yet hostile environment, the desert... Maybe that's why I feel such a connection to it (I'm giving myself a lot of credit on the beautiful part, I think)!

March 26, 2001
Glenwood Springs, CO

The security and familiarity of Glenwood Springs have encompassed me once again. I've been back for about two weeks now and have sufficiently gotten right back into the full swing of things. Although the alcohol and late nights are taking their toll. I haven't written or stretched in over two weeks and feel the need for my isolated Alaskan cabin.

Pondering what my livelihood will be this summer has been a favorite pastime lately. Maybe I'll immerse myself into my beading craft. I already know a few fairs that will be held in May, so it would be easy to sign up. Just gotta make a bunch of inventory. It's either time or money, as I always say. And right now, I've got the time.

Now, to digress a bit... Jim and I made it to Glenwood as planned. Snowboarding was fun for a few days, as was partying with old friends. But, ultimately, I had to let him go. The fact is that it was never really long-term material. It was what it was for the time that it was. No need to be dramatic about it. It just ran its course. I'm not so sure he would agree with me on all of that, but that was how it went down. He's now headed back up to Alaska to go figure out his Alaska Island Wilderness thing on his own.

Although, I have a feeling he won't be on his own for long. Only positive energy his way...

My focus for the next week or two is to spend as much quality time with Deb as possible. Sister time!! Whether or not she likes it.

April 2, 01
Glenwood Springs, CO

All the shifting energies going on lately are somewhat disconcerting. I love my life and I love traveling and I especially love Colorado. But I'm feeling uncomfortable with myself today. Why am I so closed off? It's like I'm my worst enemy. I WANT connection and intimacy, but I'm not sure I can GIVE them. It seems weird to me I have no problem having sex, but a hug sometimes feels like a violation. Jim teased me about being a "rock." Paul Simon sings it well and true: I am a rock. I am an island. But that's not what I WANT. It's definitely not for my best and highest good. There is obviously some part of me that thinks I need to protect myself from being open and vulnerable with another person. Some part of me I'm not connecting with and that I can't see or get to in order to fix it. And being a Scorpio does NOT help at all!

Maybe it has something to do with the fact that I received no physical affection as a kid. Well, that's a no brainer... And then there's being dumped by Warren in South Africa when I had no one to rely on. That was a huge scar on my psyche. Blah, blah, blah... I would like to stop complaining about these things and move PAST them; overcome the obstacles that have been placed there throughout my life in order to get to the real me. The me that is open and loving. The me that doesn't need to protect myself behind walls or rocks. The me that is no longer an island.

That might take some work, I think.

April 4, 2001
Still in Colorado

Donna and the girls are what my soul needs. Jesus, that woman...! She's a deity in and of herself! It's so fulfilling to have friends who are like soulmates. To just be completely yourself around them. And they accept you just as you are. No matter what. I come and I go. I flit here and there. I disappear for years at a time. And good old Donna Piranha is always here to welcome me with open arms. Well, maybe more with an open beer, but same idea!

It seems like she's got some shit going down in her world, too. Things in the marriage aren't great, but I'm not really sure they ever were. I always thought those two stayed together because of the girls. Those girls are so loved, and both Donna and Smitty would do anything to make their lives happy and beautiful. Including dealing with each other. I mean, they've always just been Donna and Smitty. Never really seemed overly in love or passionate. But more like friends dealing with the ride called life together. I don't know. I'll just be here for her in whatever capacity she needs me to be.

I am so utterly grateful for my friends. I've gotten to catch up with a lot of them on this excursion from Alaska and (possibly) back again. So much love. So much acceptance. So much connection.

I went to visit Teresa last week. Another one of those friendships that I am so utterly grateful for. My connection with this glorious soul has always been so cherished. Well, since college, anyway. She's definitely got some dirt on me from those years as college roommates. But our freaky souls found each other way back then and have remained connected since. We've definitely known each other in another time/place/dimension. I love her!

April 5, 2001
Glenwood Springs

Oh. My. God. The pieces are now falling into place. I just got off the phone with a wilderness lodge across the bay from Homer. It seems like I'm pretty much in if I want the job. A place called Tutka Bay Wilderness Lodge. The position is a full-time, live on premises position. During the day, I would sea kayak guide, and in the evenings, I would cook. John and Nelda are the owners, and Nelda does all the cooking. But she's needing a second hand in the kitchen for dinners. So kayak guide/cook. That's me! There's a cabin they use for employee housing, and it's shared between either 4 or 5 of us, depending on the season and the workload. Housing and food are free. I live there; they feed me. Money's okay, considering I have no overhead. And they said the tips are usually pretty good.

I sent them my resume and chatted on the phone for a bit. They told me they would let me know within a few days. I'm totally down for being a sea kayak guide in Alaska!!

On another note, Art left for a Peru trip yesterday, and Deb and I have lots of sister time now. The late-night talks have been heartwarming. She's rising to a new plateau in her soul, and I can only hope that she remains true to herself. All this bullshit about money and material objects has taken forefront to her happiness and wellbeing. That's the first time in a long time I've heard her talk like that, with some spiritual substance. For a while there, it was all about material wealth and outdoing the friends with toys and vacations. At least, that's what I saw, anyway. I'm not so sure how Art is going to fit into this new way of being for her—if he will at all. All I can do is support her right now, and that feels good enough.

Okay, time to get my ass out of bed now and face the day!

April 9, 01
Glenwood Springs

I woke up at 5 am this morning and just couldn't get back to sleep. I was wandering through the house with zillions of thoughts flying around in my head. Process, process, process...

Finally went back to sleep and started dreamtime...

I'm running from something. There's a bunch of other people running with me. But everyone is passing me, and I'm getting slower and slower. Whatever I'm running from is getting closer and closer.

I'm panicked, but no matter how hard I try, I just can't run any faster.

Dream over...

That I'm panicked in the dream is quite worrisome. I mean, maybe whatever is trying to find its way to me is about to find me. In which case, that's a good thing. But being panicked sets a very negative connotation. I'm not sure I like that!

***

Teresa departed this morning after a few nights of visiting. We got up at about 8:30 and had a lazy chat while lying around for a while before she packed up her things and hit the road. Then, basically procrastinated all afternoon about getting stuff done. Finally got my ass in gear and took the dog for a bit of a hike, and when we got back, there was a message waiting for me.

I GOT THE JOB! I got the job! I got the job! I am now an Alaskan sea kayak guide (and cook too, but whatever). Woooohoooo!!!

And there's no specific timeframe. Anytime in early May is fine. Just as I got finished jumping up and down about the news, I got a call from some guy who is working for the Aspen Ski Co and is driving up the Alaska in the next few weeks. He's got room in his car to transport my stuff back up there for $50! Divine flow, baby!! Holy SHIT!! Gratitude and abundance...

April 10, 2001
Lynn's House, still

I'm trying so hard, but I don't know how to help her. I see her crying and want to run over and put my arms around her, but she shuts me out. Please, Universe, just let her find herself. Let her be happy, with or without Art. I don't care. Just let her be happy. Now I understand how she felt all those years trying to deal with me. I pray I can give back all the goodness that she has given me.

4/12/01
Glenwood

Crying and crying and crying... I'm not sure what the hell is going on with me, but there's definitely some shifting happening. I don't even know why I'm crying. I don't feel sad. Well, not consciously, anyway. Obviously, there's some core stuff moving around. Whatever needs to be worked out is finding its way out. I guess I could call it soul level house cleaning! Whew...!

April 15, 01
Easter Sunday

Haven't written much lately, because I've been so busy doing. Connecting with Donna and the girls, seeing old friends and catching up, talking and processing with Deb.

My ticket back to Alaska is finally bought. I'll be returning to my home on April 30. After all of this back and forth, stay or go, come or leave bullshit I've been putting myself through, it somehow feels wrong to leave here. At least right now. After three weeks of checking out ticket prices, I finally bought the damned thing, and it just feels horrible. It's not a premonition feeling of something bad, just a feeling that I should be staying here, and I have no idea why. Seeing and reconnecting with friends has been wonderful, but that's a very transient thing for me, so that's not it. Maybe it's Deb. I know that she's going to need moral support, but I also know that she'll be okay without me here. I just can't pinpoint it.

But for now, the sun is shining and I'm sitting on the porch in my shorts and tank top. I'll just try to live in the present moment and enjoy it for now.

For Easter, it was a visit to Donna's for the afternoon and into the evening. We all had a great visit and ate lots of yummy food. Plenty of games were enjoyed by all and lots of loving energy. Have I mentioned how much I love my friends??

April 23, 2001
Sedona, Arizona

Once again, the journal entries have been sparse lately, and I'm feeling guilty about it. Like I haven't spoken to a good friend who has been awaiting a call from me. Silly, but true.

Deb and I are currently camped out at a little campground on a stream called Beaver Creek just outside of Sedona, Arizona. We visited a feminine vortex yesterday for most of the day and hiked around. Got lost and had to cross the stream twice. Had a divine time just enjoying the beauty of the woods and the energy. Sedona has some CRAZY energy going on! Especially at the vortex spot, of course. Even the trees here grow all twisted because of the crazy energy from the land itself.

We spent the first night in Utah outside of Moab somewhere and then got to Sedona just in time for a big snowstorm! We slept in the back of the truck in Oak Creek canyon and waited it out. Now, two days later, it's 8 am, the sun is shining down on us, and it's beautiful. Just like with life, just wait it out and it'll get better. It's so nice out that I believe the shorts and Teva's will be donned today!

Before we left, I met up with Warren–WARREN–and his little girl. And it was shockingly positive! All those years of holding onto being ditched by this South African soulmate who turned my life upside down. The love of my life. And I can joyfully say that I'M DONE with it! I still feel love for him, but it's not a chain around my heart anymore. For the first time in seven years, I am joyously over it! Watching his little girl (step-daughter, actually) playing on the swing set and thinking about the kid we could have had but chose not to... Wow... It was like a pressure release valve from my heartstrings. I love my life. Just as it is right now. And if that were our kid, my life would be extremely different. I'm still not really sure how he ended up back in Glenwood with the wife and kid and not in South Africa, but that's his choice. There's a big lesson in there for me somewhere, but I'll let that one just play itself out. The healing of my heart over that scenario is well on its way to finalization. And I'm grateful for it!

For today, in this moment, here in this amazingly beautiful and energetic place, I am asking for guidance, from all the energies/spirits/elements to show me my place in making a difference on this planet. Also, that I can open my heart to an intimate and connected relationship with the right person. I am ready.

April 25, 01
Sedona

So there I was, standing on a cliff overlooking a little stream. The red rocks glistening through the sun dazzled water. The birds chirping and twitting around. And it hit me like a brick in the chest. I'm not ready to go back to Alaska yet. The tears came pouring down. And I just let the feeling flow through me, asking for it to keep on flowing out of me. We are driving back to Colorado from this desert oasis of Sedona tomorrow, and I will be on a plane bound for the north on Sunday. For the first time in three years, I don't want to go back to Alaska right now. I'm not even excited about the kayak gig at the moment.

Deb and I are connecting so well and have been for a month now, and I feel like I'm leaving my best friend just when she needs me the most. But Art comes back on Sunday, and she has to run this course on her own. It's not mine to figure out for her. This is going to be really hard for her, but I know she'll make whatever choice is necessary for her happiness. So, why do I have such a heavy heart???

Shit... I'm going to go collect firewood and try to make some sense of my head and heart.

April 28, 01
Glenwood Springs

It is my last day in Glenwood for this time around. My last month has been so filled with love and connection, and I am so beyond grateful! My feeling of not wanting to go back has somewhat dissipated, and I'm now looking forward to seeing Boomer, being back in my cabin again, and going out to cheap, shitty Mexican food with Hank (AKA my redneck friend).

The prospect of kayaking and cooking all summer in the middle of the Alaska wilderness is exciting. But I would like to have a more environmental focus for the future. Some way that I feel that I can give back instead of just consume, like a greedy human. What form will that take? Where will it lead me? When will it happen? Will I be sharing it with someone special? Presently, there are no answers to those questions. But I'm looking forward to the future.

Alaska seems like such a far-off reality right now, though. It's weird, almost like a time warp or something. Maybe just a shift. After the past four months of so many different paths and adventures...

April 30, 01
35,000 Feet

Salt Lake City is my stopover until I take off for Seattle on the next flight. I'm stuck in the middle seat on a very full plane. Ick. I never knew Seattle was such a popular place. My panicky feeling about leaving diminished when we got into Denver last night. I'm still quite uncertain where that came from or what it was there for, but it almost had me sick to my stomach on the drive through the mountains. I was so extremely unsettled! But it's gone now, and I'm thankful for that. Now, visions of Alaska are filling my head. Tomorrow. Only one more night, and I'll be in my little cabin with my very missed dog, Boomer! I'm interested to see what happens with Josh and I. And looking forward to a summer living off the grid, at the base of a mountain range, on the Alaskan coastal waters, being paid to take people kayaking every day!

As I ponder the last 8 months of my life, I simply have to smile. Sometimes my life is so crazy that it feels like I'm an observer watching a movie. It's a very fast-paced movie, and sometimes I'm not really sure where it's going. But that's the point! I get to choose between going with the flow or creating my own reality. Or maybe that's just it, the divine sweet spot in between the two. I love being in charge of my own life. I love being a strong, independent woman who can make her own decisions. I love knowing I get to call the shots of my own story. I don't do it because it's empowering. But because I do it, I am empowered.

Staring out of the plane window, my next steps are wide open. Only I can create the next scene. Admittedly, my insides are a bit in turmoil between complete excitement and utter apprehension. I am learning, over the years, that this juxtaposition of emotions is my ultimate motivation. I choose to embrace it and edge towards complete excitement for the moment! On towards my future...

Dedications

There are so many people to whom I owe much gratitude and thanks. And there is no way that my memory or my writing skills will do them all the justice they deserve. None of us are alone, and none of our accomplishments are done singularly. Mostly, my writing is in dedication to all the women out there, both young and old, who may somehow be motivated by my memories and the style in which they are written. As a strong, independent woman, I am well-aware that those traits are not always taken as positive attributes to the female gender. No matter, I hope each and every one of us wears our badges of strength and independence proudly. Every single woman on this planet deserves recognition for her strength, in some way. I am here to give you that recognition. Stand proud. Don't take anyone's shit. Love with everything you have. And teach your children to do the same.

To the people of Cuba, I am awe-struck by your happiness. You are, by far, the happiest people I have ever encountered and I am so grateful for the genuine welcome into your country, your homes, and your hearts. Many, many, many thanks goes to my partner, Jay. His unquestionable belief in me has become my rock and I am humbled by it.

And, of course, I have immense gratitude for the people I met along my travels. Fellow travelers that have become life-long friends are the best motivation a writer could ask for! Elizabeth, I am looking forward to us sharing these stories for decades to come.

With great love, affection, and thanks to everyone who shared a bit of their souls to help add to my story... To all of those explorers and adventurers out there, keep on keeping on.

CPSIA information can be obtained
at www.ICGtesting.com
Printed in the USA
BVHW031740100721
611635BV00007B/307